# TABLE OF CONTENTS

4

Las vegas skyline

Las Vegas Boneyard Museum

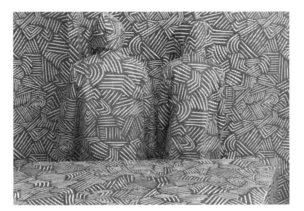

Go for a fun photo ops adventure at Paradox Museum

Embark on a time travel adventure at Titanic: The Artifact Exhibition

# INTRODUCTION

## Welcome to the City of Lights

Welcome to Las Vegas, the land of shimmering lights, boundless entertainment, and the thrilling promise of endless possibilities. In the heart of the Mojave Desert, Las Vegas pulses with a joyful, vibrant energy, an optimism that seems to defy the arid landscape that surrounds it.

In this remarkable oasis, where dreams are woven into the very fabric of the streets, you'll find a place unlike any other on Earth. Las Vegas!!!

This city is quite a spectacle, a grand performance that unfolds day and night. It's a place where the Eiffel Tower and Venice's romantic gondolas coexist on the same vibrant boulevard and where extravagance knows no bounds. It is also the place where the line between reality and fantasy blurs into a dazzling tapestry of neon and dreams.

Yearly, Las Vegas opens its arms to more than 42 million visitors, beckoning them to enter a world of wonder and excitement. This city has not only claimed its throne as one of the top three destinations in the United States but has also earned its place among the most famous resort cities on the global stage.

Las Vegas is a city that thrives on captivating the senses, where every corner exudes an aura of awe-inspiring amazement. It's a place where the night sky is alive with the vibrant glow of a thousand signs. The air in Las Vegas is constantly infused with the electric charge of possibilities.

I found myself utterly fascinated by this incredibly unique city. I mean, where else can you stroll down a street and visit both the Eiffel Tower and

Venice's gondolas? But as I delved deeper into exploring Las Vegas, both on the iconic Las Vegas Strip and beyond, questions started to brew. Why is Las Vegas the nation's gambling mecca? How did it come to be this way, right here in the heart of the Mojave Desert?

Join me on a journey through the streets of this unique city, where we'll unravel the mysteries of why Las Vegas is the nation's gambling mecca, and how it evolved into the dazzling, enigmatic metropolis it is today. But before we delve into the world of casinos and high stakes, let's first understand why a city chose to rise from the desert sands, defying the odds and creating a haven of excitement and entertainment in a place where water is scarce, and the sun reigns supreme. Welcome to Las Vegas, where the adventure of a lifetime awaits, and every moment is a chance to experience the extraordinary.

## Unveiling the Sin City: A Brief History

First, let's get a bit of background. Las Vegas welcomes a whopping 40 million visitors every year, making it one of the top tourist destinations in the USA. Now, it's often dubbed "Sin City," and that reputation might have you picturing it as an adult-oriented haven for gambling and drinking. While that's certainly a big part of what Vegas offers, there's more to it than meets the eye.

Vegas has also transformed into a major business destination, playing host to world-renowned conventions that draw in excess of a hundred thousand attendees. You might be familiar with events like the Consumer Electronics Show, which attracts massive crowds. But there are lesser-known but equally significant conventions like the World of Concrete.

And speaking of concrete, let's not forget about the incredible hotels and resorts that grace the Las Vegas landscape. They're truly something to behold. Vegas has mastered the art of creating stunning accommodations that cater to a wide range of tastes and budgets.

Sin City has quite the tale to tell!

In 1844, Spanish explorers gave it the name Las Vegas, which means "The Meadows." It wasn't much more than a dusty spot in the desert until 19th-century explorer John C. Fremont came along in 1844. Then, we had some Mormon missionaries from Utah try to make it their home, but they found the desert weather a bit too harsh.

Things started picking up when Nevada became a state in 1864. Las Vegas became a crucial pit stop for trains traveling between Los Angeles and Salt Lake City. This brought the Mormons back to town, and they became an essential part of the community.

On May 15, 1905, Las Vegas officially became a city. Senator William Andrews Clark held a land auction that day. Then, on March 16, 1911, Las Vegas was officially incorporated. But here's the twist: Nevada banned gambling in 1910, causing some financial hiccups after World War I.

In 1926, a highway connected Vegas to California, but the city lacked any real tourist attractions or landmarks. So, it wasn't exactly a tourist hotspot yet.

Now, things started to get a little shady. Las Vegas began to gain a reputation for its ties to organized crime and, well, illegal fun. During the Great Depression, they began building the Hoover Dam, and people flocked to Vegas for work. They had to live in government-controlled Boulder City to keep those Prohibition-era rules in check, but many found ways to spend their paychecks in Vegas.

In 1931, they loosened marriage and divorce laws, and by 1933, gambling became legal once again after the end of Prohibition. That was like opening Pandora's Box for local business folks, investors from the Mormon community, and some big players in organized crime. They saw a chance to entertain the mostly male dam workers by building casinos and theaters.

After the construction wrapped up, a lot of workers moved on, leaving Vegas with an uncertain future. To drum up some business, they introduced Helldorado Days, a marketing gimmick to attract visitors and celebrate their wild-west heritage. But it wasn't enough, and drawing tourists remained a challenge.

Then, in 1935, the Hoover Dam started attracting tourists, and it brought electricity to downtown Las Vegas. The city's western-themed Fremont Street, named after the explorer John C. Fremont, became famous as "Glitter Gulch" thanks to its bright lights.

In 1941, El Rancho Vegas opened its doors as the first resort on the famous Las Vegas Strip. This success led to more construction, and when Los Angeles started cracking down on illegal gambling in the early 1940s, criminals turned to nearby Sin City.

Mobsters like Benjamin "Bugsy" Siegel and Moe Dalitz opened their casinos, marking the era of organized crime ownership. Siegel introduced some Hollywood glamor with the Flamingo in 1946, and Dalitz earned the nickname "Mr. Las Vegas" by opening the Desert Inn in 1950. More mob-owned casinos followed, often with funding from unexpected sources like Jimmy Hoffa's Teamsters and, believe it or not, even the Mormons.

Following a federal inquiry, organized crime's grip on legalized gambling seemed secure from government intervention. Oddly enough, even nuclear testing in 1951 became a tourist attraction and transformed Vegas into a more family-friendly destination.

By the mid-1950s, over 8 million people were flocking to Vegas each year, drawn by gambling, entertainment, and star-studded shows featuring the likes of Elvis, Liberace, and the Rat Pack.

During this period, Vegas also began breaking the color barrier in entertainment, thanks to pressure from the NAACP and prominent black entertainers. The Kennedy administration played a role in diminishing mob influence in the city.

The late 1960s saw Howard Hughes, the eccentric businessman and aviator, make his mark by buying up properties and eliminating organized crime's presence. He gave Vegas a sophisticated makeover, and legitimate corporations gradually took over ownership.

The 1970s brought explosive population growth to Vegas, despite Atlantic City offering another gambling paradise by 1976. In the 1980s, some deadly hotel fires and a resurgence of mob activity cast a shadow on Vegas. But the 1990s brought a renaissance with the construction of larger and more extravagant hotels and casinos, like Steve Wynn's Mirage, the Luxor, and the new MGM Grand.

By the end of the century, over 37 million people were visiting Las Vegas each year. Regardless of its multiple reinventions, one thing remained certain: what happens in Vegas, stays in Vegas.

# What is New in Las Vegas?

## The Sphere

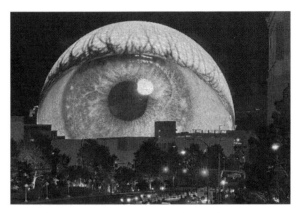

The Sphere, also known as MSG Sphere, is an innovative spherical entertainment arena newly constructed in Paradise, Nevada. Aptly positioned just near the Las Vegas Strip and close to the Venetian resort, this groundbreaking project was developed by Madison Square Garden Entertainment and it opened its doors on 29th September 2023.

As reported by CNN, the Sphere stands prominently in the Las Vegas skyline, resembling a massive spacecraft that exudes an air of mystery during the day. However, when night falls, it transforms into a luminous spectacle akin to the Earth seen from space.

This architectural marvel proudly holds the title of the world's largest spherical building, featuring an impressive 500-foot diameter and soaring to a towering height of 218 feet. Notably, its theater boasts the world's highest-resolution wraparound LED screen, providing an unparalleled visual experience. The Sphere's exterior is adorned with a staggering 1.2 million LEDs, each about the size of a hockey puck, which can be programmed to display dynamic imagery on a massive scale, also earning the distinction of being the world's largest LED installation of its kind.

With a seating capacity of 18,500, the Sphere is meticulously designed to offer an immersive entertainment experience like no other. Key highlights include an advanced 16K resolution wraparound LED screen, cutting-edge speakers employing beamforming and wave field synthesis technologies, and the remarkable ability to create 4D physical effects.

The Sphere has so much promise. Its unwavering commitment to delivering top-tier entertainment, encompassing a wide spectrum of events ranging from concerts and sporting matches to prestigious award ceremonies is also notable. Let's delve deeper into some of its extraordinary features:

16K Resolution Wraparound LED Screen: Inside the Sphere resides the world's largest and highest-resolution LED screen, capable of crafting immersive visuals that transport audiences to entirely new realms.

Beamforming and Wave Field Synthesis Speakers: Redefining audio technology, the Sphere boasts a cutting-edge sound system that can precisely direct sound to specific areas within the venue, ensuring an unparalleled auditory experience.

4D Physical Effects: Adding another layer of immersion, the Sphere has the capability to generate physical effects such as wind, rain, and vibrations, elevating the overall experience for attendees.

As if that is not enough, the Sphere's exterior will be a canvas for captivating animations and imagery that change throughout the day and night, sometimes aligning with the seasons. For instance, it could metamorphose into a colossal pumpkin for Halloween or transform into a winter wonderland for Christmas, adding to the venue's allure.

The Sphere looking like a pumpkin...

## The B-52s at The Venetian Resort Las Vegas

The B-52s are an iconic rock band known for their classic 60s style. With a career spanning three decades, they've garnered a dedicated fan base. Their live performances continue to showcase their original enthusiasm and prioritize a laid-back and enjoyable atmosphere.

Here are some upcoming concerts for The B-52's in Las Vegas:

- Friday, April 12, 2024, at the Venetian Theatre at the Venetian Resort, Las Vegas.
- Wednesday, April 17, 2024, at the Venetian Theatre at the Venetian Resort, Las Vegas.
- Friday, April 19, 2024, at the Venetian Theatre at the Venetian Resort, Las Vegas.
- Saturday, April 20, 2024, at the Venetian Theatre at the Venetian Resort, Las Vegas.

Price: US $45.41 – US $256.83

## Voltaire Belle de Nuit

The Venetian is all set to debut its new nightclub, Voltaire, on November 3rd, and they've already locked in Kylie Minogue as the headliner. The theme is going to be heavily influenced by Couture, with a modern Art Deco fantasy vibe. Interestingly, they've brought in costume designers to help design the interior, so expect a swanky and aesthetically pleasing atmosphere. Kylie Minogue's shows are in high demand and selling out fast.

Speaking of the Venetian, they recently opened Juliet Cocktail Room. It's worth noting that they've maintained a similar decor style to The Dorsey, but they've added pianos and introduced a refreshed cocktail menu.

Furthermore, the Venetian is also giving their sportsbook a makeover with a remodeling project in the works.

They've also introduced a robot bartender here, similar to the one you'd find at Planet.

## A New Vanderpump Restaurant at Flamingo?

A new Vanderpump restaurant concept is set to open at the Flamingo. This will be the third Lisa Vanderpump restaurant and bar, alongside Vanderpump Cocktail Garden at Caesars and Vanderpump A Paris. Currently, it's being referred to as the "Purple Zebra" as a code name. There's speculation that it might have an Art Deco theme, but some are hoping for a tropical theme that would complement the Flamingo's vibe. Regardless, Lisa Vanderpump is known for creating stunning restaurants.

*Swingers at Mandalay Bay*

Mandalay Bay has exciting plans to construct an adults-only golf course called "Swingers," set to open in 2024. This 21-and-up destination will span a generous 40,000 square feet and feature five unique crazy golf courses. What adds to the fun is the idea of cocktails being served from caddy carts and the inclusion of food trucks. It's shaping up to be a fantastic place for adults to enjoy some recreational activities.

## Getting the Most Out of Your Las Vegas Adventure

- Choosing The Right Time to Visit

Choosing the right time to visit Las Vegas largely depends on your preferences. If you enjoy taking a dip in swimming pools and don't mind the scorching heat, summer is the ideal season for you. The summer season in Vegas is synonymous with excellent pool weather, but it can get very hot.

However, if you prefer milder temperatures, then winter is your best bet. Just keep in mind that Vegas can surprise you with cooler mornings and evenings during the winter season. Therefore, packing some warm clothing, such as jackets, is essential. Many people underestimate how chilly it can get, with temperatures occasionally approaching freezing.

One valuable tip is to plan your visit when there are no major events or conventions in town. Las Vegas thrives on such gatherings, and during these times, the city can be more crowded. You can maximize your enjoyment of the city by checking the event calendars and choosing quieter periods. If you find yourself needing warmer clothes during your winter visit, remember that the stores on the Las Vegas Strip tend to be high-end luxury retailers like Dior and Louis Vuitton. The wisest choice is bringing your own affordable jacket from home.

- Eating in Las Vegas

Las Vegas is a haven for food enthusiasts. Prepare yourself, (and your stomach) for a diverse culinary scene. Buffets are a Vegas specialty, and one of the standout options is the Bacchanal Buffet at Caesars Palace. The great thing about Vegas buffets is that you can make reservations, sparing you the hassle of waiting in long lines. Buffets are worth checking out in advance.

Bacchanal Buffet distinguishes itself with a trend that's catching on in Vegas – smaller plates showcasing unique items like dragon fruit and mango smoothies. While many fantastic restaurants in Vegas require reservations, some of the best are tucked away on higher floors, accessible via elevators. For example, Bouchon at the Venetian is a gem that you won't stumble upon while wandering the casino floor.

If you're looking for a quick, budget-friendly meal, consider trying the sandwiches at Planet Hollywood's Earl of Sandwich. The food here is a far cry from mass-produced buffet fare; it's genuinely delicious. The roast pork from the Chinese section, for instance, surpasses expectations. Unlike other buffets that provide small dessert plates, Bacchanal offers full dinner-sized plates for desserts, making it a dessert lover's paradise.

Keep in mind that indulging in more than one buffet a day can lead to overindulgence and discomfort, so stick to just one. Also, be aware of time limits at some buffets due to increased demand and reservations. At Bacchanal, there's a 90-minute limit.

- Drinking in Las Vegas

After gambling, drinking fuels much of the Vegas experience. You'll find drinks everywhere, but they can be quite expensive, especially at bars on the Strip. To save on beverages, consider purchasing drinks at CVS or Walgreens. On the Strip, you can enjoy your beverages in most areas, but carrying a plastic cup can be handy. Plastic cups are readily available at most hotels, allowing you to switch your drink from glass to plastic for on-the-go convenience. If you're looking for affordable alcoholic beverages or non-alcoholic drinks, check out the ABC stores, which are scattered along the Strip and inside the Planet Hollywood Miracle Mile Shops.

Another important thing to note is that smoking is allowed in many places in Las Vegas, which may affect both smokers and non-smokers. While some casinos offer designated no-smoking sections, the Park MGM has even gone entirely smoke-free. If you're a smoker, you'll find ample opportunities to light up, including cigars and, notably, marijuana, which is legal in the city. However, smoking marijuana in public spaces is technically not permitted, although enforcement can be lax.

- The Las Vegas Strip

The Las Vegas Strip is truly a world of its own. Imagine hotels that take the shape of pyramids, castles, and even feature erupting volcanoes out front. It's a destination like no other, and while many have attempted to replicate Vegas's charm around the world, nothing quite compares to the original.

Now, let's focus on the most famous part of Las Vegas: Las Vegas Boulevard. This bustling street stretches for nearly 50 miles, but the real star of the show is the Las Vegas Strip, a four-mile stretch that runs from Mandalay Bay to the Stratosphere. It's packed with so much to see and do that many visitors find themselves never leaving the Strip during their entire stay.

But here's an intriguing tidbit about the Las Vegas Strip—it's not technically in Las Vegas itself. The city of Las Vegas comes to an end, and the Strip is located in the unincorporated towns of Paradise and Winchester. So, if you happen to come across addresses mentioning Paradise, Nevada, or Winchester, Nevada, don't worry; you're still right in the heart of Las Vegas. This distinction might come in handy when you're using Google Maps to navigate your way around this fascinating city.

- Downtown Las Vegas

Many folks affectionately refer to downtown as the true heart of Vegas. It's where the city's story began, the original settlement, and the original gambling hub before the glitzy Strip stole the limelight.

The core of downtown is centered around Fremont Street, especially the famous Fremont Street Experience. This 'experience' is a covered area spanning five blocks, adorned with a stunning display of 24 million LED lights. When night falls, it comes to life with captivating shows on the hour, running from dusk until midnight.

Downtown has its enthusiasts who appreciate its more grounded vibe, but it's not everyone's cup of tea. Some argue that it's quite a distance from the Strip, about a $30 cab ride away, and complain about the smokiness of the casinos. However, if you're a fan of slot machines, downtown might just be your paradise. Here you will come across some of the best odds in town. And if you enjoy table games, you'll find some thrilling action, particularly at the Circa Hotel.

- Family Getaways

Las Vegas is often associated with its adult-oriented attractions, earning the nickname "Sin City." However, in recent years, the city has been actively catering to families, making it a more family-friendly destination. Many hotels, resorts, and casinos are targeting families, offering a variety of activities and amenities suitable for all ages.

You'll find that many properties, like the New Horseshoe Hotel Las Vegas (formerly Bally's), have invested in family-friendly features such as arcades, bowling alleys, and miniature golf courses. This trend is prevalent in Vegas right now, with an increasing number of options for family entertainment.

While the city is known for its topless pool day clubs, there are far more family-friendly swimming pools to choose from. For instance, Mandalay Bay boasts a massive wave pool that's a hit with kids.

When it comes to allowing kids in Vegas, most places, including casinos, permit children to pass through the casino floor. However, individuals under the age of 21 are not allowed to linger or gamble on the casino floor. If you plan to visit with young children, it's advisable to avoid the Strip and Fremont Street Experience after 9:00 PM when the atmosphere becomes more adult-oriented and lively. During the daytime and early evening, staying within the resort properties on the Strip can provide a family-friendly experience.

It's worth noting that two hotels in Las Vegas, the **Circa Hotel Downtown** and the **El Cortez**, are exclusively for adults aged 21 and above. This means that children are not allowed to stay or enter these hotels. If you're seeking a kid-free environment, these are two options to consider.

Therefore, while Las Vegas still retains its reputation for adult entertainment, it's evolving into a more family-friendly destination with a wide range of options for visitors of all ages.

- Explore Nearby Neighborhoods

Let's discuss some nearby neighborhoods that might pique your interest as a visitor.

First is Summerlin, one of Vegas's more upscale areas. Here, you'll discover the JW Marriott, the Red Rock Casino, and the stunning Red Rock recreation area. If you're a fan of hiking, this is a fantastic place to indulge in your passion, especially during the cooler winter months.

Venturing a bit further out, you'll come across Lake Las Vegas, conveniently situated on the route to the Hoover Dam. It's a unique neighborhood nestled around a picturesque lake. Lake Las Vegas is exuding a charming Mediterranean town ambiance. There are a couple of hotels, including a Weston, so this location is an ideal choice if you're seeking a peaceful retreat away from the city's hustle and bustle. However, do keep in mind that if you're looking for shopping or other amenities, you'll need to make a roughly 10-minute drive to access them.

But please, don't think these are the only gems Las Vegas has to offer. It's a sprawling city with plenty more to explore beyond the bustling Strip and downtown. Nonetheless, if it's your first time here, these are excellent areas to start your adventure.

- Getting Around

If you're arriving in Las Vegas by plane, you'll likely land at Harry Reid International Airport, which was previously known as McCarran International Airport. It's essentially the same airport but with a recent name change. This airport is quite sizable, boasting more than a hundred gates and serving around 50 million passengers annually.

One of the quirkiest things about Las Vegas's airport is that you can actually try your luck with slot machines while waiting for your flight or during a layover. Another noteworthy fact is that it's the busiest airport in the United States that isn't considered a hub for major legacy carriers like American, United, or Delta. Instead, you'll find a significant presence of budget carriers, with Southwest leading the pack, followed by Spirit, Allegiant, and others in that category.

Now, let's talk about getting from the airport to the famous Las Vegas Strip. Most travelers prefer taking a taxi or a ride-sharing service. Taxis have fixed fares divided into three zones, typically ranging from $20 to $30, depending on payment method and your destination on the Strip. If you're heading downtown, it might reach a maximum of around $40, assuming you hit some traffic. Without traffic, the ride takes about 15 minutes, but during peak congestion, it could stretch to 45 minutes.

Now, let me tell you about shared ride shuttles at the airport, where you share a van with others to save some money. My advice: skip it. These shuttles tend to be time-consuming and not worth the hassle. However, if you're feeling like a high roller, consider arranging a limousine service right at the airport. Several limo companies are available, which can be especially convenient for larger groups.

Another option is renting a car. There are 11 rental car companies located in the consolidated Rent-A-Car Center, but keep in mind you'll need to take a shuttle from the airport to get there, which takes about 10 minutes. If you're renting from one of the off-airport companies, you'll need to catch a second shuttle to reach them, but honestly, it's usually not worth the extra trouble. Stick with the rental companies at the Rent-A-Car Center. However, I must mention that if you're staying on the Strip, renting a car isn't typically necessary, and I'd advise against it due to potential traffic and parking challenges.

For those who prefer driving themselves, you can use your own vehicle. I personally drive in too. Alternatively, you can arrange for a driver through many of the major resorts, though this option tends to be on the pricier side. If you do decide to drive, be prepared for traffic, especially on Interstate 15 and along the Strip. Weekends, in particular, can see congestion, turning what's usually a 15-minute drive on a weekday into over an hour on a Friday or Saturday. Plan accordingly.

Now, here's a local tip: the pros and Vegas residents usually avoid driving directly on the Strip. Instead, they opt for the roads just adjacent to it, either along Interstate 15 or the opposite side of the Strip. These side streets can save you time unless, of course, you're eager to soak in the bright lights of the Strip.

Oh, and if you're driving and looking for free parking on the Strip, you can find it at Tropicana, TI, Venetian/Palazzo, Wynn/Encore, Resorts World, Sahara, and the Stratosphere.

- Pedestrians in Vegas

Despite Las Vegas being situated in the desert with scorching summer temperatures, it's surprisingly pedestrian-friendly. The city has invested in wide sidewalks and pedestrian bridges that conveniently link the various hotels, so you often don't even need to cross the street.

However, I'd like to offer a word of caution, especially for your first day here: don't overdo the walking. It's a common mistake visitors make, and they end up with painful blisters, which can put a damper on the rest of their trip. Take it easy and pace yourself. The Strip may only stretch four miles from end to end, but you'll be walking through the casinos as well, which adds to the mileage as you explore everything this vibrant city has to offer.

**The Deuce Bus**

Now, if you're looking for alternative ways to get around, consider hopping on the Deuce Bus. This double-decker bus is a cost-effective option, with fares at six bucks for two hours, eight bucks for an entire day, or $20 for a three-day pass. You can purchase tickets from machines along the Strip or onboard. The Deuce Bus covers the entire length of the Strip, all the way to downtown. Keep in mind that it can get stuck in Strip traffic on busy nights, and it makes numerous stops, which can extend your travel time. Nevertheless, it's a great way to enjoy some sightseeing from the second deck as you watch the city's dazzling lights.

- **The Las Vegas Monorail**

Another option, albeit one with a limited lifespan, is the Las Vegas Monorail. Enjoy it while it lasts because they have plans to dismantle it in the not-so-distant future. This monorail primarily connects the east side of the Strip hotels to the convention center. This one is handy for convention-goers. It's also useful if you're going from, say, MGM Grand to the Sahara. However, for hotels on the other side of the Strip, such as Bellagio and Caesars Palace, the monorail won't get you there. Additionally, if you're staying at MGM Grand, it can take around 15 minutes to navigate through the hotel just to reach the monorail, so it might not be the best choice for short distances.

Seasoned Vegas visitors know about the interconnected interior hallways that link many of the hotels and casinos. For example, if you want to move from Paris to Horseshoe, you can use the interior hallway at the rear to seamlessly transition between the two hotels. These hallways can save you time and energy, especially if you're navigating between nearby properties.

- Hotel Tip

Choosing the right hotel in Las Vegas is a crucial part of planning your trip, and I have some tips to help you make the best choice. First, I strongly advise against simply picking the cheapest hotel you can find. Vegas does offer some unbelievably low rates, but more often than not, you'll end up regretting your decision. The hotel rates in Vegas can fluctuate wildly. For instance, during the holiday season, you might spot rates as low as $19 a night at places like Excalibur. However, during special events like a football game at Allegiant Stadium, those same rates can skyrocket to over $500 a night. So, it's essential to consider the timing of your visit, avoiding conventions and major sporting events if possible to secure more budget-friendly rates.

One smart move is to join the Players Clubs, such as Caesars or Mlife with MGM. Once you're a member, be sure to log in with your Players account when you're searching for rooms and rates. You'll often discover cheaper rates and special offers when you're logged in.

In general, room rates tend to be lowest on weekdays, especially from Monday to Wednesday. Conversely, Friday and Saturday nights are typically the most expensive. Additionally, hotels located closer to the center of the Strip, like Caesar's Palace and Bellagio, tend to be pricier. As you move farther down the Strip or away from its center, you'll find more affordable options.

- Resort Fees

Keep an eye out for those sneaky resort fees. Almost every Vegas hotel charges these extra fees on top of the room rate. These fees can be as high as $50 or more per night, so factor them into your budget. However, if you're a member of certain Players Clubs and have elite status, some hotels may waive these fees for you. For example, Mlife often does this for gold members. Remember to use your Players Card when you're gaming to enjoy special perks and save money on future trips to Vegas.

If you prefer a quieter experience or want to avoid the casino scene, consider staying at a non-casino hotel. While most of the major Strip hotels have casinos, there are exceptions like the Waldorf Astoria in CityCenter, which doesn't have a casino. Another excellent option is the Marriott Grand Chateau, a Marriott timeshare hotel located just a block off the Strip. Staying at hotels like these, slightly off the beaten path, can be significantly more cost-effective. Plus, parking is often free or reasonably priced, and resort fees are either low or nonexistent. This is particularly advantageous if you'll be driving.

One last thing, when you encounter showgirls on the Strip or costume characters, remember that they rely on tips. If you take a picture with them, it's customary to offer a tip in return. The same applies to the costume characters you'll come across during your Vegas adventure.

- About Gambling in Las Vegas

Las Vegas is renowned for its gambling opportunities, which are widespread throughout the city. You'll encounter gambling not only on the famous Strip and downtown but also in unexpected places like gas stations, bars, and even the airport. However, it is paramount that you familiarize yourself with the rules of the games before participating. Avoid playing any game you do not fully comprehend. Most major casinos offer complimentary lessons to educate you on the various games available.

Additionally, I recommend enrolling in the Players Clubs, as I mentioned earlier. These clubs offer various benefits, such as priority access to buffets and complimentary meals. Be sure to take full advantage of these perks.

When engaging in gambling activities, it's essential to establish a strict financial limit. Choose an amount that you are comfortable with, and consider it your maximum spending limit. If you happen to reach that limit and incur losses, resist the temptation to chase your losses by continuing to gamble. Pursuing such a course can lead to financial troubles rather than a prosperous outcome, and it's advisable to exercise responsible gambling practices.

In Las Vegas, it's important to be prepared to offer tips as service providers often rely on them. It's a good practice to have some cash on hand, particularly in the form of one-dollar bills. You can easily obtain these by using the ticket machines on the casino floor. Simply break a $20 bill, and the machine will provide you with both fives and ones.

It's worth noting that the ATMs within the casinos can be quite expensive due to additional fees, so having cash on hand is advantageous. Additionally, finding bank ATMs can be a bit challenging, so it's wise to plan accordingly and carry some cash for your convenience.

- Taking Day Trips

Las Vegas serves as a great starting point for exploring some fantastic day trip destinations. Here are a few popular ones:

Hoover Dam: A short 45-minute drive from Las Vegas, the Hoover Dam is a marvel of engineering. You can take a guided tour inside to learn about how it generates electricity and its history.

Grand Canyon: The Grand Canyon is one of the most famous natural wonders in the world. There are different options for day trips, including tours to the West Rim on Native American land, which features the famous Skywalk, or the Grand Canyon National Park, a longer four-hour drive from Las Vegas. While it's possible to do it in a day, it makes for a long trip.

Zion National Park: Located about two to three hours from Las Vegas, Zion National Park offers stunning red rock landscapes, hiking trails, and a unique opportunity to explore the great outdoors.

Death Valley National Park: Another captivating natural destination, Death Valley National Park, is a two to three-hour drive from Vegas. Here, you can witness unique geological features, extreme desert conditions, and breathtaking landscapes.

These day trips offer a great way to experience the natural beauty and diverse landscapes surrounding Las Vegas. If you do decide to go to any of these locations, your visit to the Vegas area will be even more memorable. Make sure to plan accordingly and check for tour options if you prefer not to drive yourself.

## Mistakes to Avoid When Visiting Las Vegas

When you're heading to a new place like Las Vegas, it's natural to encounter a few hiccups along the way. Here are some common mistakes to steer clear of during your Vegas adventure:

**Airport Transportation:** Your journey starts at the airport, and getting to your hotel smoothly is key. Cabs have set rates now, so no more worries about getting long-hauled. But keep an eye on Uber and Lyft prices; they can surge during conventions and events. Compare them on your phone to save some bucks. If ride-sharing is pricier, opt for a cab, but carry some cash to avoid card fees.

**Slot Machine Denominations**: Slot machines can be tricky. Before you press that button, check the denomination. Some high-value machines aren't in high-limit rooms. A small mistake could cost you big – like my friend who bet $70 instead of $7. Start with one-cent machines if you're new to gambling to avoid accidental overspending.

**Jaywalking No-No**: It's tempting to follow the crowd when people start crossing on a red light, but busy traffic areas can be risky. Jaywalking or crossing outside of designated areas can result in hefty fines. Stick to crosswalks and obey traffic signals to stay safe.

**Food Portions:** Portions in Vegas are enormous. Don't overorder; you can always grab a snack later. The heat can reduce your appetite more than you think.

**Room Security:** Lock your hotel room door securely. Some unauthorized individuals may lurk around hallways and stairwells, checking for unlocked doors. Use your in-room safe for valuables like laptops, jewelry, and extra cash.

**Hailing a Cab:** You can't hail a cab in the middle of the street on the Vegas Strip. Cabs have designated pickup and drop-off points. With Uber, the rules are different, and pickup locations can vary, so ask hotel staff for guidance.

**Street Offers**: Be cautious of accepting items from strangers on the street, even if they claim it's free. Some street performers or salespeople can be aggressive. If needed, politely say you're a local to deter them.

**Shots and Sharing**: Shots in Vegas tend to be large. Ask for an extra cup and share with a friend to avoid overindulging.

**Distance Deception:** What seems nearby might be quite far in reality. Don't underestimate the size of the Strip. Walking from one end to the other can take hours. Consider taking an Uber or cab if you're heading further than a couple of properties away.

**Free Trams:** Take advantage of the free trams available on the Strip. They can help you navigate large distances without spending anything and save your feet from excessive walking.

Utilizing the three free trams that travel between Mandalay Bay and Treasure Island will allow you to explore most of Las Vegas Boulevard while limiting your walking.

Remember that these trams are not the official Las Vegas Monorail system that runs along the eastern side of the strip. The three free trams are operated independently and supported by the various casinos they connect, in contrast to the Las Vegas Monorail, which requires tickets.

**Security Deposits:** Hotels often place a hold on your credit card for incidentals. Be aware that this amount can vary, so don't risk overdrawing your card by not accounting for it. It's typically released upon check-out.

**Resort Fees:** Most hotel rates in Vegas don't include taxes and resort fees. These fees can add up, so confirm the total cost, especially if you're booking through third-party websites or packages.

Tipping is customary in Las Vegas. In restaurants, 20% is a common tip. On the casino floor, tip for drinks based on what you're betting, with a minimum of $2 per drink. Remember to tip bell services and valet attendants as well.

Avoid touching items in the mini-fridge. The shelves and items are often on weighted sensors, and moving them may result in unexpected charges. If this happens, inform the front desk to rectify it.

Pool Preparations: When heading to the pool, minimize the stuff you bring with you. Consider using a waterproof case to protect essential items like phones and keys, ensuring you can fully enjoy your swim without worrying about your belongings.

# PREPARING FOR YOUR LAS VEGAS ADVENTURE

## Weather and Seasons: What to Expect

Las Vegas has four distinct seasons throughout the year, and each one offers a unique atmosphere and range of activities. Here are some seasonal forecasts and recommendations for the best travel times for different categories of tourists:

- March to May:

Moderate to warm temperatures, with highs between 21°C and 32°C (70°F to 90°F).

The spring is a fantastic time to venture outdoors and go sightseeing. The great weather is ideal for enjoying a variety of outdoor activities, wandering the Las Vegas Strip, and going for walks in Red Rock Canyon.

Travelers who value a comfortable temperature and outdoor activities should choose this option.

March to May Festivals;

**Electric Daisy Carnival (EDC)**: Held in May, EDC is one of the world's largest electronic dance music festivals, featuring top DJs and elaborate stage productions.

**Viva Las Vegas Rockabilly Weekend**: Celebrate the rockabilly culture with music, car shows, and vintage fashion in April.

**Great Vegas Festival of Beer**: Beer enthusiasts can enjoy craft beer tastings and live music in April.

- Summertime (June through August)

Summer is warm and dry, with daily highs frequently topping 100°F (37°C). Pool parties, indoor attractions, and nighttime entertainment are the mainstays of summer in Las Vegas. The city's thriving nightlife and air-conditioned casinos draw a lot of tourists.

Best for people who like hot weather, pool parties, and nightlife.

June to August Festivals:

**World Series of Poker (WSOP):** Taking place from late May to mid-July, WSOP attracts professional and amateur poker players from around the globe.

**EDC Week:** A series of pool parties and nightclub events leading up to Electric Daisy Carnival in May.

**Las Vegas Market:** Held in July, this is one of the largest home and gift trade shows in the United States.

- September to November:

The temperature will be warm during the day and cold at night, with highs between 80°F and 95°F (27°C and 35°C).

The frigid winter offers a welcome equilibrium in the fall. Outdoor pursuits like golfing, hiking, and visiting the local natural wonders are great at this time of year.

Best for Golfers, outdoor enthusiasts, and people who like milder weather.

September to November Festivals:

**iHeartRadio Music Festival:** This two-day music festival in September features top artists from various genres.

**Life is Beautiful Festival**: A multi-genre music and arts festival held in September, featuring music, art installations, and culinary experiences.

**Las Vegas Food & Wine Festival**: Wine and dine at this festival in October, featuring gourmet food and wine tastings.

- Winter (December through February)

The weather is mild with daytime highs of 50 to 60 degrees Fahrenheit (10 to 15 degrees Celsius), but cooler evenings.

Shows, concerts, and fine dining are all excellent indoor entertainment options during the winter. Additionally, you might benefit from winter sales at retail locations.

Winter is best for vacationers looking for indoor entertainment, holiday celebrations, and thrifty shoppers.

December to February Festivals:

**National Finals Rodeo (NFR):** In December, the NFR brings together top rodeo athletes for a championship event.

**New Year's Eve Celebrations:** Las Vegas is famous for its extravagant New Year's Eve celebrations on the Strip.

**Chinese New Year Parade and Festival:** Celebrate the Lunar New Year in January or February with a vibrant parade and cultural performances.

- Best Time for Various Traveler Types

**Outdoor adventurers:** The spring and fall seasons offer pleasant weather for going on hikes, biking tours, and discovering natural wonders.

Fans of the city's dynamic nightlife can enjoy pool parties and other summertime activities during this season.

Budget travelers should take advantage of the lower hotel prices and wonderful retail opportunities that winter brings.

**Families:** With beautiful weather and outdoor activities, spring and fall are ideal seasons for families.

Tourists: While any season can be used for touring, spring and fall provide the most pleasant weather for getting around the city.

## Planning Your Trip: How

Getting to Las Vegas can be done through various means of transportation, catering to different types of travelers. Here are some options:

- By Air:

For Long-Distance Travelers: If you're coming from another state or country, flying to McCarran International Airport (now known as Harry Reid International Airport) is the most common option. This airport is well-connected to major cities worldwide.

Domestic Travelers: Most major U.S. cities offer direct flights to Las Vegas, making air travel convenient for domestic travelers.

International Travelers: International visitors can fly into Las Vegas through connecting flights at major U.S. airports.

- By Car:

Road Trippers: If you enjoy road trips, you can drive to Las Vegas. It's easily accessible by major highways like Interstate 15. This option is ideal for travelers who want to explore the surrounding areas or have flexibility in their schedule.

RV Travelers: Many RV parks and campgrounds are available for those traveling in recreational vehicles.

- By Bus:

Budget Travelers: Several bus companies offer affordable long-distance routes to Las Vegas. These can be a cost-effective option, especially for travelers on a tight budget.

Regional Travelers: Some travelers may opt for regional buses or shuttle services if they are coming from nearby cities or states.

- By Train:

Train Enthusiasts: Amtrak offers train service to Las Vegas from various cities. While it may not be the fastest option, it can be a unique and scenic way to travel.

- By Motorcycle:

Adventure Seekers: Motorcyclists often enjoy the open roads leading to Las Vegas. The area offers picturesque routes and opportunities for exploration.

- By Bicycle:

Cyclists: For the adventurous and physically fit, cycling to Las Vegas is possible. However, it's essential to plan your route carefully, considering the long distances and varying terrain.

- By Private Jet:

Luxury Travelers: For those seeking a luxurious travel experience, private jets can be chartered to arrive directly at Las Vegas' private terminals.

- By Cruise Ship (Indirect):

Cruise Lovers: While Las Vegas is not a coastal city, some cruise lines offer pre- or post-cruise packages that include transportation to the city. These cruises typically depart from nearby ports like Los Angeles or San Diego.

Considerations:

1. Depending on where you're starting your journey, consider the distance and duration of travel when choosing your transportation method.
2. Your budget can play a significant role in deciding how to get to Las Vegas. Compare the costs of different options, including flights, bus tickets, gas, or RV rental fees.

3.  Evaluate how much time you have for your trip. Some transportation methods may be faster, while others offer a more leisurely journey.
4.  Personal preferences, such as comfort, adventure, and flexibility, can also influence your choice of transportation.

## Packing for Fun and Style

Packing for a trip to Las Vegas, known for its vibrant nightlife, entertainment, and desert climate, requires some thoughtful planning to ensure you're prepared for a mix of activities. Here's a guide on what to pack for a fun and stylish Las Vegas trip:

1. Clothing:

Casual Wear: Pack comfortable clothing for daytime activities, such as sightseeing, shopping, or lounging by the pool. T-shirts, shorts, sundresses, and lightweight pants are suitable.

Dressy Outfits: Las Vegas is known for its nightlife and upscale restaurants. Bring stylish outfits for evenings out, including cocktail dresses, dress shirts, slacks, and fashionable shoes.

Swimwear: If your hotel has a pool or if you plan to visit pool parties, pack swimsuits, cover-ups, and sunscreen.

Outerwear: Evenings can be cooler, so bring a light jacket, cardigan, or shawl.

Comfortable Shoes: You'll do a lot of walking, so pack comfortable walking shoes or sandals. For nightlife, consider dressy shoes that match your outfits.

2. Accessories:

Sunglasses: Protect your eyes from the desert sun while looking stylish.

Hat: A stylish sun hat not only adds flair to your outfit but also shields you from the sun.

Jewelry: Bring accessories to elevate your evening attire.

3. Toiletries:

Sunscreen: The desert sun can be intense, so pack sunscreen with a high SPF.

Hydration: Stay hydrated with a refillable water bottle.

Toiletries: Bring your preferred toiletries, including shampoo, conditioner, and skincare products.

Medications: If you take prescription medications, don't forget to bring them along.

4. Electronics:

Chargers: Pack chargers for your smartphone, camera, and any other devices you'll use.

Camera: Las Vegas offers plenty of photo-worthy moments, so don't forget your camera.

Power Bank: Ensure your devices stay charged throughout the day.

5. Documents and Essentials:

Identification: Carry a valid ID, driver's license, and passport if you plan to visit bars or clubs.

Travel Documents: Have your travel itinerary, hotel reservations, and any necessary travel documents.

Wallet: Bring cash, credit/debit cards, and a secure way to carry them.

Health Insurance: If you're traveling from abroad, ensure you have appropriate health insurance coverage.

Travel Adapter: If you're from outside the U.S., bring a travel adapter for your electronic devices.

6. Entertainment:

Reading Material: If you enjoy reading, bring a book or e-reader for downtime.

Music and Headphones: Create a playlist for your trip and enjoy music on the go.

Travel Games: Consider bringing small travel-sized games for entertainment.

7. Miscellaneous:

Reusable Shopping Bag: Useful for carrying souvenirs or groceries.

Backpack or Day Bag: A small backpack can be handy for carrying essentials during the day.

Swimsuit Bag: Pack a separate bag for wet swimwear to avoid dampening your other belongings.

8. Personal Style:

Las Vegas is a city where you can express your personal style. Feel free to bring statement pieces or clothing that makes you feel confident and stylish.

## Budgeting for Your Sinful Escapade

Budgeting for a trip to Las Vegas, often referred to as "Sin City," is crucial to ensure you enjoy your sinful escapade without breaking the bank. Here are some budgeting tips to help you plan your Las Vegas adventure:

Set a Total Budget:

Determine the total amount you're willing to spend on your trip, including accommodations, transportation, food, entertainment, and shopping.

Break Down Your Expenses:

Create categories for your expenses, such as:

Accommodations: Research hotel rates and choose a place that fits your budget.

Transportation: Consider flight or road trip costs, airport transfers, and local transportation expenses.

Food and Dining: Allocate funds for meals at restaurants, buffets, and snacks.

Entertainment: Plan for shows, attractions, and nightclub cover charges.

Shopping and Souvenirs: Set aside money for shopping sprees and souvenirs.

Miscellaneous: Include expenses like tips, travel insurance, and unforeseen costs.

Consider staying at hotels off the Strip or in downtown Las Vegas, which tend to be more budget-friendly than upscale resorts.

Look for deals, discounts, and package offers when booking accommodations.

Opt for budget-friendly dining options like food courts, local cafes, and off-Strip restaurants.

Take advantage of happy hour specials and dining deals during non-peak hours.

Set a daily gambling budget and stick to it. Avoid chasing losses by knowing when to stop.

Join casino players' clubs to earn rewards and discounts on dining and entertainment

Prioritize the attractions and shows you want to see, and allocate funds accordingly.

Look for discounts and package deals for Las Vegas shows and experiences.

Enjoy free attractions like the Bellagio Fountains and the Volcano at the Mirage.

Plan your shopping budget and avoid impulsive purchases.

Seek out outlet malls and discount stores for affordable shopping options.

Compare flight and transportation options to find the most budget-friendly choice.

Use rideshare services like Uber or Lyft for short trips around the city.

Be aware of resort fees that many Las Vegas hotels charge. Check if they are included in your booking.

Use ATMs sparingly to avoid high fees. Bring some cash with you from home.

Keep a record of your daily expenses to stay within your budget. There are mobile apps that can help you do this.

Set aside a small amount as an emergency fund for unexpected expenses.

Las Vegas offers numerous free and low-cost attractions, such as exploring the Strip's architecture or hiking in nearby natural parks.

It's easy to overspend in Las Vegas, especially with its lavish offerings. Stay disciplined and avoid overindulging.

Planning your trip in advance allows you to take advantage of early booking discounts and better control your spending.

Be prepared to adjust your budget if needed. Sometimes, opportunities for savings or unexpected expenses can arise.

# THE THRILLS OF THE STRIP

## *The Iconic Las Vegas Strip: A Stroll Through Neon Paradise*

You'll find a plethora of captivating things and activities to enjoy on the Las Vegas Strip. The strip  stands at the heart of all things entertaining. Las Vegas excels at ensuring you have a fantastic time, providing a wide range of attractions, including complimentary performances and thrilling amusement rides.

Explore the Las Vegas Strip with this tour that covers all the must-see spots. You can begin your journey at any point along the Strip, but I suggest starting at the  Mandalay Bay Resort and Casino  and wrapping up at the STRAT. This way, you'll experience all the major attractions in a logical order.

- The Welcome to Fabulous Las Vegas Sign

South end of Las Vegas Blvd (Las Vegas Boulevard) and Mandalay Bay Road.

Start your journey with a classic photo op at the iconic "Welcome to Fabulous Las Vegas" sign, which marks the beginning of the Strip. This is a must-visit spot to capture the true essence of Las Vegas.

- Mandalay Bay

Even if you're not staying here, you should check out the beach and pool area. The Shark Reef Aquarium is also located at Mandalay Bay. Mandalay Bay is themed like the exotic South Seas. I recommend paying a visit to the Dolphinaris, a dolphin and other marine mammal habitat. You can even interact with the dolphins by swimming with them and learning to train them.

- Luxor

Visit the Egyptian-themed Luxor. Admire its iconic pyramid-shaped design, which is based on the Luxor pyramid in ancient Egypt. There are also other Egyptian-themed attractions, such as a Sphinx replica, a Luxor-themed pool complex, and a range of Egyptian-themed restaurants and cafes.

When you're at Luxor, I recommend visiting Bodies: The Exhibition. It's a fascinating showcase featuring 13 whole-body specimens and over 260 organs and partial body specimens, providing an educational experience like no other. Just note that the last admission to the exhibit is one hour before closing time.

While you're there, make sure to also explore Esports Arena Las Vegas. This multi-level space is a dream come true for any dedicated gamer. They've got a jaw-dropping 50-foot LED video wall where you can catch all the tournament action of the day. You can even rent out rooms equipped with top-notch computers to play games with your friends. Plus, there's a gamer-inspired menu curated by the renowned celebrity chef José Andrés. Whether you're into Rocket League or League of Legends, you won't run out of games or tournaments to enjoy here. And don't forget, they even have a ladies' night – it's a gamer's paradise!

While you're at Luxor, don't miss the Titanic Exhibition. This remarkable exhibit showcases over 250 authentic artifacts and stunning replicas from the renowned ship, providing a truly immersive experience that brings history to life. Just keep in mind that the last admission to the exhibit is one hour before closing, so plan your visit accordingly to make the most of this incredible journey through time.

Check out the Luxor Skywalk too, it is  a glass-bottom walkway with amazing views of the Las Vegas Strip and adjacent desert. The Luxor has a number of shows available, including magic shows, comedy shows, and concerts.

- Excalibur

Excalibur's intriguing medieval theme pervades the entire resort. A stroll through their enormous lobbies will immerse you in a world inspired by the fabled Camelot castle. If you're looking for a thrill, check out The Tournament of Kings, a spectacular jousting tournament dinner show held in Excalibur's very own King Arthur's Arena. Knights on horseback, spectacular jousting contests, and a variety of other medieval-themed entertainment are featured in the presentation. Also, don't miss The

Excalibur Arcade, a large gaming room loaded with a variety of video games, pinball machines, and other arcade games.

- New York-New York Hotel and Casino

Here, you'll see an amazing replica of the Statue of Liberty and even get to ride a thrilling roller coaster. New York-New York is well-known for its enthralling New York City-themed design, which includes replicas of famous Big Apple monuments such as the Statue of Liberty, the Empire State Building, and the Brooklyn Bridge. This hotel doesn't only look good; it also has a slew of New York-themed activities, including a heart-pounding roller coaster and a detailed reproduction of Times Square. There are also a number of New York-themed restaurants and pubs to visit.

Don't miss out on The Big Apple Coaster, a roller coaster that wraps its way around the outside of the hotel tower, providing amazing views of the Las Vegas Strip and the surrounding desert. Catch the complimentary New York-New York water display, which graces the hotel's front every half hour. For your delight, this stunning spectacle mixes flowing fountains, captivating music, and colorful lights.

While you're exploring New York-New York, I highly recommend making a pit stop at Hershey's Chocolate World. This delightful store is a chocolate lover's paradise. You'll find everything from classic Hershey's chocolate bars and jumbo-sized chocolate syrup bottles to Reese's peanut butter cups, Ice Breakers, Jolly Ranchers, and Twizzlers.

Be sure to head downstairs too where you will  discover a colorful wall of Hershey's Kisses dispensers, perfect for filling up your bag with these iconic treats. In addition to these tempting treats, Hershey's Chocolate World also sells souvenirs and gifts, including clothing, coffee mugs, and other fun items. It's conveniently located right in front of the New York-New York hotel-casino.

- Park MGM and Aria Resort and Casino

Park MGM Las Vegas is a smoke-free resort. It is well-known for its modern aesthetics and significant emphasis on the arts. Don't miss out on the opportunity to explore a broad collection of art works, including the spectacular 40-foot-tall sculpture known as Bliss Dance, which is prominently positioned at the property's core. You can also enjoy entertainment alternatives like the Dolby Live theater, where you can see amazing concerts and live performances at Park MGM.

Aria is ideally positioned about 5 minutes from Park MGM. Notably, Aria integrates a variety of environmentally friendly technologies, such as a rainwater collecting system and a solar power arrangement. The affluent Crystals retail mall is nearby, providing good chances for high-end shopping.

- Bellagio

I recommend taking full advantage of the magical Bellagio experience. Start by taking a stroll through the alluring Bellagio Conservatory, where you can see the spellbinding Bellagio Fountains performance. Every 15 to 30 minutes, these enthralling performances provide a lovely spectacle in the evenings.

Don't forget to stop by the Bellagio Conservatory & Botanical Gardens, a sizable 14,000 square foot botanical garden decorated with an assortment of plants and flowers. The conservatory is a perennial favorite among visitors because of its extraordinary seasonal modifications, which guarantee there is always a new theme to appreciate.

I also recommend spending some time perusing the Bellagio Gallery of Fine Art. This gallery houses an ever-changing collection of top-notch artwork that is sure to inspire. It is located inside the Bellagio hotel-casino at the intersection of Flamingo Road and the Las Vegas Strip.

And if you get the chance, be sure to check out the bronze circus figures by renowned artist Richard MacDonald. These fascinating sculptures can be found outside the foyer of the "O" Theatre at Bellagio as well as inside the lobby of the hotel-casino. Additionally, Gallery Row, conveniently situated just across the bridge from Crystals at CityCenter, is home to another outstanding exhibition of Richard MacDonald's artwork.

Think about going for a swim at the Bellagio pool complex to cool off from the heat of Las Vegas. It's the ideal spot to unwind and escape the desert heat with four welcoming swimming pools, two relaxing whirlpools, and a variety of other pleasant water attractions.

- The Cosmopolitan

At The Cosmopolitan, you'll be greeted by its swanky atmosphere and mesmerizing art exhibits. The Cosmopolitan is designed with cutting-edge architecture, emphasis on art and culture, and lively, energetic atmosphere.

You'll come across a wide variety of art installations as you explore the hotel, which give the area a certain appeal. Watch for Jeff Koons' impressive neon cactus sculpture, which he created with skill. Don't miss the chance to experience a mesmerizing video art display created by James Turrell as well. The Cosmopolitan's atmosphere is significantly improved by these creative components.

The Cosmopolitan also provides a variety of entertainment opportunities to suit different tastes. Particularly notable as a center for live performances are the Chelsea Theater's concerts, comedies, and other events.

Check out The Ice Rink at The Cosmopolitan, a lovely recreation of the famous Boulevard Pool into a winter wonderland, if your schedule permits. Ice skating, relaxing by the fire pits, savoring warm drinks, indulging in s'mores, and even watching holiday movies are all available here.

- Caesars Palace

Take a leisurely stroll through Caesars Palace's Forum Shops, a shopping paradise with a variety of premium shops and top-notch eateries. Be sure to experience the luxury of the casino floor while you're there, where excitement is palpable.

Don't forget to take in the free Fall of Atlantis fountain show as you wander. This captivating production tells the mythical story of Atlantis using lifelike animatronic figures and amazing effects. It's a captivating show that will enthrall spectators of all ages.

The Escape Room, conveniently located inside the Forum Shops at Caesars Palace, is a great option if you're ready for some exciting adventures with your buddies. Recall that reservations are required for this fun experience.

- The Mirage

Be sure not to miss the legendary volcano show right outside The Mirage; just make sure to check the showtimes. While you're at The Mirage, take some time to explore the lush tropical atrium inside, a hidden oasis of greenery and tranquility.

The spectacular Volcano at The Mirage has been enhanced with two volcano systems, a serene lagoon, and fire shooters that can shoot flames as high as 12 feet into the night sky. You can catch this fiery spectacle on the hour at 7:00 p.m., 8:00 p.m., 9:00 p.m., 10:00 p.m., and 11:00 p.m. It's a captivating show that's bound to leave you in awe.

You'll find The Mirage hotel-casino conveniently located on the iconic Las Vegas Strip, situated between the intersections of Flamingo and Spring Mountain Road.

- The Venetian and The Palazzo

Don't miss the chance to experience the romance of a gondola ride at The Venetian. As you glide along the peaceful waters, serenaded by the gondoliers with soothing Italian melodies, you'll truly feel transported to the charming canals of Venice. Located at the Venetian hotel-casino, right at the intersection of the Vegas Strip and Spring Mountain Road, this gondola ride is a delightful and entertaining way to spend your time.

In the spirit of Italian tradition, there's a lovely custom where couples can share a kiss under each bridge you pass beneath, symbolizing good luck. And believe me, there are plenty of bridges along the way. But it's a sweet and heartwarming experience, and you won't mind it one bit – moments like these remind us of the special connection with our loved ones.

The gondola ride offers both indoor and outdoor options. Indoors, you'll drift through the Grand Canal Shoppes, this way, you get to admire the beautifully designed Italian-inspired architecture and the illusion of a blue sky-painted ceiling. Outdoors, you'll glide along a picturesque lagoon at the front of the hotel, treating you to breathtaking views of the Las Vegas Strip. Just keep in mind that outdoor rides might be affected by inclement weather.

Each gondola can accommodate up to four passengers, so you might share the experience with another couple. Even if you're not on a romantic date, it's a wonderful way to take a break from the bustling city and truly escape for a little while.

While you're here, there are a couple of other exciting attractions you should check out. Madame Tussauds Las Vegas showcases over 80 incredibly lifelike wax figures of famous celebrities from the worlds of film, television, and music. It's quite a surreal experience, and you'll be amazed at just how realistic these wax replicas look. It's a fun and unique way to "meet" your favorite stars, even if they are made of wax.

If you're up for some excitement, immerse yourself in the interactive world of PanIQ escape rooms, located inside the Grand Canal Shoppes. These escape rooms offer thrilling 45 or 60-minute adventures that will challenge your wits and creativity.

And if you have a passion for music, I recommend indulging in some stylish karaoke at KAMU Ultra Karaoke, also within the Grand Canal Shoppes. Sing your heart out in a luxurious setting and make some unforgettable memories with friends.

Make sure not to miss the breathtaking Palazzo Waterfall Atrium at The Venetian. As soon as you step inside, you'll be transported to a world of natural beauty, and all the raucous activity of the Las Vegas Strip will fade away.

The grand multi-story atrium is a true marvel, featuring a beautiful waterfall, a domed skylight that bathes the space in natural light, and a dazzling array of exotic flowers – some with names that are probably a tongue-twister.

What makes the Palazzo Waterfall Atrium even more special is its seasonal transformation, which includes festive touches for Chinese New Year.. It is Located at the entrance to the Grand Canal Shoppes at The Venetian

- The Fashion Show Mall

Be sure to explore the fabulous retail offerings at the Fashion Show Mall, a huge shopping center that boasts a unique retractable runway and a plethora of dining choices. It covers an impressive 2 million square feet. The Fashion Show Mall is also home to an extensive collection of both boutique and chain stores, so you know that it is one of the top shopping destinations in the city. On select weekends, you can even enjoy live runway shows, adding an extra layer of excitement to your shopping experience.

You'll find this shopping haven conveniently located at the corner of Las Vegas Boulevard and Spring Mountain Road. It is easily accessible and a fantastic place to indulge in some retail therapy and savor delectable dining options.

- Treasure Island (TI)

I recommend taking a journey into the thrilling world of Marvel's superheroes and villains with an immersive adventure at the Avengers S.T.A.T.I.O.N. headquarters. You can find this exciting experience inside Treasure Island, conveniently situated on the third floor, just above CVS. It's a must-visit for fans of the Marvel cinematic universe, offering an unforgettable exploration of your favorite characters and their incredible stories.

- The LINQ Promenade

I suggest you check out Brooklyn Bowl at LINQ. This place isn't your typical bowling alley; it's a whole different ball game on the Las Vegas Strip.

Brooklyn Bowl is a fantastic fusion of a bowling alley, a concert venue, and a restaurant all rolled into one exciting package. It is equipped with 32 state-of-the-art Brunswick lanes, complete with massive high-def screens above the pins, it's a unique bowling experience. You can even have restaurant-style service right at your lane and relax in a stylish bowlers' lounge with comfy chesterfield sofas. And if you're bowling during a concert, you'll groove to live music from some of the hottest bands in town (remember, you'll need show tickets to bowl during a concert).

The LINQ is also where you'll find The High Roller, the largest observation wheel in the United States, boasting 28 transparent pods.

- The Stratosphere

The Stratosphere Hotel and Casino is home to the tallest observation tower in the United States. At 1,150 feet, it offers breathtaking panoramic views of the Strip and the desert. Don't miss the thrilling rides atop the tower. Also, there's "Insanity - The Ride." This one is a real heart-pounding adventure as it dangles you over the edge of The STRAT while spinning you at speeds of up to three Gs. The views of the dazzling Las Vegas Strip are incredible, and the ride back down is an exhilarating rush. You can find this adrenaline-pumping experience at The STRAT Hotel, Casino, and Skypod, just north of where the Vegas Strip intersects with Sahara Avenue.

For the true thrill-seekers, "SkyJump Las Vegas" is an absolute must. It's essentially a "controlled free fall" from the 108th floor of the tower, and the sensation is simply indescribable. The moment you take that leap is something you'll remember forever.

Now, if you're looking for a unique and exciting ride, "X-Scream" is worth a shot. It is a giant teeter-totter combined with a roller coaster, and you've got a pretty good idea of what this one's like. It's a wild ride that'll get your heart racing.

There's also the "Big Shot." Trust me, you won't want to miss this one. It catapults you to a staggering 1,049 feet above the ground atop The STRAT's Skypod. Then, you experience an incredible free fall that makes you feel like you're weightless. It's an adrenaline-pumping adventure you won't soon forget.

- Flamingo Las Vegas resort.

Flamingo Wildlife Habitat: Take a peaceful break at the Flamingo Wildlife Habitat, a free outdoor exhibit located at the Flamingo Las Vegas resort. Here, you can observe flamingos, birds, turtles, and fish in a serene environment. It's open daily from 8:00 AM to 5:00 PM.

- The High roller

The High Roller is a colossal Ferris wheel situated in the heart of the Las Vegas Strip, specifically at the east end of The LINQ Promenade. This remarkable attraction boasts the title of the largest observation wheel in the United States, featuring 28 transparent pods, each capable of holding 40 passengers.

Here are the essential details:

**Address: 3545 S Las Vegas Blvd, Las Vegas, NV 89109, United States**

**Coordinates: 36°07'03"N 115°10'05"W / 36.117402°N 115.168127°W**

Hours of Operation:

Monday to Sunday: 12:00 PM to 12:00 AM

The High Roller stands at an impressive height of 550 feet with a diameter of 520 feet, making it an iconic part of the Las Vegas skyline. It officially opened to the public on March 31, 2014, earning the distinction of being the tallest Ferris wheel in the world at the time. This captivating attraction is owned and operated by Caesars Entertainment, offering visitors an unforgettable ride and stunning views of the Las Vegas cityscape.

- Immersive Disney Animation

Immersive Disney Animation offers a captivating family-friendly experience right on the Las Vegas Strip. Here are the key details:

The Lighthouse Artspace, inside The Shops at Crystals

Lighthouse Artspace, 3720 S Las Vegas Blvd, Las Vegas, NV 89109, United States.

Phone: 1-866-983-4279.

Hours of Operation:

Monday to Sunday: 10:00 AM to 7:45 PM

Step into a whole new world of magic as you explore the enchanting world of Disney animation. This is an immersive experience that promises fun and wonder for visitors of all ages. It will be a fantastic addition to your Las Vegas adventure.

- The Strat Tower And Thrill Rides

The STRAT Tower Observation Deck and Thrill Rides offer an exhilarating way to experience Las Vegas from above. Here are the key details:

Phone: For inquiries and bookings, you can contact them at 1-866-983-4279.

Location: The STRAT Tower Observation Deck is situated at The STRAT Hotel, Casino & Tower, just north of the intersection of the Vegas Strip and Sahara Avenue.

Coordinates: 36.147386°N 115.155389°W.

Address: 2000 S Las Vegas Blvd, Las Vegas, NV 89104, United States.

Hours of Operation:

Monday to Sunday: 2:00 PM to 10:00 PM

Here, you can view the city in a breathtaking 360-degree panorama. As the tallest freestanding observation tower in the United States, it promises awe inspiring views of the Las Vegas skyline. You can also enjoy thrilling rides that will add an extra dimension of excitement to your visit. Don't miss the chance to experience the city from new heights at The STRAT Tower.

- The Big Apple Coaster

Experience the thrill of the Big Apple Coaster at New York-New York Hotel & Casino in Las Vegas. Here are the details:

Phone: For inquiries and more information, you can contact them at 1-866-983-4279.

Coordinates: 36°6'7"N 115°10'29"W.

Address: 3790 South Las Vegas Boulevard, Las Vegas.

The Big Apple Coaster is located on the second level inside the New York-New York hotel-casino. You will find this casino at the south end of the Las Vegas Strip, where Las Vegas Boulevard meets Tropicana Avenue.

Hours of Operation:

Monday and Tuesday and Wednesday and Thursday: 11:00 AM to 11:00 PM

Friday: 11:00 AM to 12:00 AM

Saturday and Sunday: 11:00 AM to 12:00 AM

Prepare for towering drops and exhilarating loops. You will also be rewarded with breathtaking views of the Las Vegas Strip as you take on the Big Apple Coaster's exciting ride

- Immersive Van Gogh

Explore the world of art like never before at the ORIGINAL Immersive Van Gogh Exhibit in Las Vegas. Here are the details:

Price: Tickets start at $39.

Location: The exhibit is situated at the Shops at Crystals, adjacent to ARIA Resort & Casino, located at 3720 S Las Vegas Blvd, Las Vegas.

Phone: For inquiries and additional information, you can contact them at 1-866-983-4279.

Experience Details:

Experience: Immerse yourself in the beauty and emotions of one of history's most influential artists, Vincent van Gogh, in a completely new and immersive way.

Hours of Operation:

Monday: 11:00 AM to 6:00 PM

Tuesday, Wednesday, Thursday and Friday: 1:00 PM to 8:00 PM

Saturday: 1:00 PM to 9:00 PM

Sunday: 11:00 AM to 6:00 PM

- Eiffel Tower Viewing Deck

Experience the romance and grandeur of the Eiffel Tower replica at Paris Las Vegas. Here are the details:

Price: Tickets start from $27.

Location: You can find the Eiffel Tower viewing deck at Paris Las Vegas, situated just south of the intersection of the Vegas Strip and Flamingo Road.

Phone: For inquiries and additional information, you can contact them at 1-866-983-4279.

Experience Details:

Experience: From the rivets in its beams to its glass elevators, this replica of the Eiffel Tower encompasses the same charm, appeal, and unique quality that is captivating but not easy to describe as the original, offering breathtaking views of the Las Vegas Strip.

Hours of Operation:

Monday: 5:00 PM to 12:00 AM

Tuesday: 5:00 PM to 12:00 AM

Wednesday: 5:00 PM to 12:00 AM

Thursday: 5:00 PM to 12:00 AM

Friday: 5:00 PM to 12:00 AM

Saturday: 5:00 PM to 12:00 AM

Sunday: 5:00 PM to 12:00 AM

Address: 3655 Las Vegas Blvd S, Las Vegas, NV 89109, United States

- Museum Of Illusions

The Museum of Illusions in Las Vegas is a fascinating attraction that features a captivating collection of rooms, installations, and images that challenge your perspective and play with your senses. It's a place where you'll discover that things are not always as they appear.

Location: The museum is conveniently located on the Las Vegas Strip, situated between the Cosmopolitan and the Shops at Crystals.

Hours of Operation: You can explore the Museum of Illusions during the following hours:

Monday: 10:00 AM to 12:00 AM

Tuesday: 10:00 AM to 12:00 AM

Wednesday: 10:00 AM to 12:00 AM

Thursday: 10:00 AM to 12:00 AM

Friday: 10:00 AM to 12:00 AM

Saturday: 10:00 AM to 12:00 AM

- Shark Reef Aquarium

Explore one of the most extensive aquatic exhibits at the Shark Reef Aquarium, starting at just $29. This remarkable attraction at Mandalay Bay boasts a diverse collection of over 2,000 aquatic species, including awe-inspiring sharks and exotic fish.

Location: You'll find the Shark Reef Aquarium at the Mandalay Bay resort-casino, conveniently situated near the intersection of the Vegas Strip and Hacienda Avenue.

Hours of Operation: Plan your visit during the following hours:

Monday: 10:00 AM to 8:00 PM

Tuesday: 10:00 AM to 8:00 PM

Wednesday: 10:00 AM to 8:00 PM

Thursday: 10:00 AM to 8:00 PM

Friday: 10:00 AM to 8:00 PM

Saturday: 10:00 AM to 8:00 PM

Sunday: 10:00 AM to 8:00 PM

- Fly Linq

Experience the thrill of flying 12 stories above The LINQ Promenade with the Fly LINQ Zipline, starting at just $45.

Location: You'll find this exhilarating adventure at The LINQ Promenade.

Hours of Operation: Plan your high-flying adventure during the following hours:

Monday: 2:00 PM to 10:00 PM

Tuesday: 2:00 PM to 10:00 PM

Wednesday: 2:00 PM to 10:00 PM

Thursday: 2:00 PM to 10:00 PM

Friday: 2:00 PM to 10:00 PM

Saturday: 2:00 PM to 10:00 PM

Sunday: 2:00 PM to 10:00 PM

## Dining in Style: Restaurants Along the Strip

Without a doubt, Las Vegas is a food lover's paradise, and it caters to every taste and budget imaginable. If you're craving the elegance of a Michelin-starred dining experience with stunning panoramic views or searching for hidden culinary treasures tucked away in unassuming strip malls, Las Vegas will deliver it to you. One thing I truly appreciate about this city is its culinary diversity, ensuring that even the most pickiest of eaters will discover a dish to love.

- Gordon Ramsay Steak at Paris Las Vegas

Gordon Ramsay is a culinary icon, and if you're a fan of his and appreciate top-notch American grill and steakhouse cuisine, then Gordon Ramsay Steak at Paris Las Vegas is an absolute must-visit. Located on the first floor of the Paris Vegas Hotel, this restaurant offers a dining experience that's truly worth every penny, even if it falls in the $$$$.

You can expect nothing less than high-quality beef, with the famous Beef Wellington being one of Gordon Ramsay's personal favorites. The restaurant's design beautifully blends traditional London style with a modern flair, setting the stage for a memorable meal. The menu is a delight with offerings like King Crab Legs and Sticky Toffee Pudding.

The meal here is a culinary spectacle. So, if you're ready for a dining experience that's both theatrical and incredibly delicious, this is the place to be. Las Vegas is all about indulgence and creating unforgettable memories, and Gordon Ramsay Steak fits right into that picture.

- Amalfi at Caesars Palace.

Bobby Flay is a culinary genius! If you're a fan of his skills and want to savor some exceptional Italian cuisine, then you must dine at Amalfi at Caesars Palace. This restaurant, brought to you by the renowned celebrity chef himself, brings the flavors of the Italian coast right to your plate in Las Vegas. With a focus on seafood, you'll find delectable dishes like Squid Ink Pasta and Wood Grilled Swordfish. And the highlight? The Crudo Bar, where you can personally choose your fish from a seafood display that's like a scene from an Italian market. The warm Mediterranean-inspired decor adds to the immersive experience. I must confess, it makes me feel like I'm dining on Italy's sun-drenched coast. It's definitely a must-visit for Italian food enthusiasts. Just be prepared as you will have to spend up to $$$!

- Le Cirque

Now, let me introduce you to a dining gem: Le Cirque. It is nestled within the Bellagio, this restaurant is impressive. The interior looks like a whimsical, vibrant circus tent straight out of the past. What makes it even more special is that it's owned by the renowned Maccioni family, known for their legendary expertise in the culinary world.

Le Cirque offers an exceptional French dining experience that's nothing short of extraordinary. Their tasting menu is filled with flavors, featuring premium ingredients like caviar, and truffles. Complementing these delectable dishes is an extensive wine list, and the service is nothing less than impeccable. I recommend reserving a window table to enjoy breathtaking views of the Bellagio fountains. It's a dining experience that combines culinary excellence with visual spectacle.

Just a heads-up, Le Cirque is indeed a fine dining establishment, and it falls into the $$$$. This restaurant is celebrated for its upscale French cuisine, offering a top-notch culinary experience in the heart of Las Vegas. So, be prepared to indulge in a dining adventure that's not just delicious but also a bit more luxurious on the wallet.

- Chin Chin

If you're craving some delicious Chinese food while in Las Vegas, you should definitely check out Chin Chin at the New York-New York Hotel and Casino. This restaurant offers a variety of delectable Asian cuisine that's sure to satisfy your taste buds. They apply an open kitchen concept, so you can even watch as your meal is expertly prepared. I love this interactive element. And be sure not to miss out on their famous banana spring rolls for dessert – they're a real treat! Plus, Chin chin is  reasonably priced, meaning it's an excellent choice for a satisfying yet casual meal.

- Ramen Ya

Ramen Ya is an excellent spot, especially if you're a fan of ramen. Located at the intersection of Flamingo and Las Vegas Blvd near the Paris, it offers both great prices and delicious food. During my visit, I noticed the restaurant was bustling with Japanese patrons enjoying their ramen, which is always a good sign.

On my first visit, I tried the beef curry dish, and it was not only flavorful but also served in a generous portion. What really stood out was the fried chicken ramen, a unique choice that I found absolutely delightful. The restaurant itself is cozy and intimate, and the staff is incredibly friendly and accommodating. Ramen Ya is a small gem with fantastic service and, as you've experienced, outstanding food. I wholeheartedly recommend it for any ramen enthusiast.

- Secret Pizza at The Cosmopolitan

Secret Pizza is an absolute hidden gem tucked away at The Cosmopolitan. It's a casual New York-style pizza joint with a unique twist – there's no prominent signage out front, making it challenging to spot if you're just passing by. To discover this culinary treasure, you'll need to follow the intriguing path on the third floor of The Cosmopolitan, adorned with album covers featuring legends like Frank Sinatra and Elvis. Plus Secret Pizza is cheap too and you can spend as low as $10!

While  you traverse this musical hallway, you'll eventually stumble upon a tiny, standing-room-only eatery. At the walk-up counter, they serve up fresh slices of classic pizza varieties like pepperoni, cheese, and veggie. If you're in the mood for a whole pizza to enjoy in your room, they'll whip one up for you in about 15 minutes. While waiting, you can have a blast at the brightly-colored pinball machine – a fun way to pass the time.

Remember that Secret Pizza doesn't open until 11 am, and before that, the record-lined hallway is blocked off by a sliding door. So, when you're at The Cosmopolitan, be sure to explore this fantastic hidden spot for a taste of New York-style pizza with a side of mystery!

- The Wicked Spoon Buffet at The Cosmopolitan

The Wicked Spoon Buffet at The Cosmopolitan is definitely worth a visit. While it's a bit disappointing that they don't offer dinner throughout the week, their brunch is truly fabulous. I love their approach of serving individual portions, allowing you to savor a diverse range of dishes.

I found everything on the menu to be delightful, with a special shout-out to the crab legs – they were a real treat. To sweeten the deal, they offer bottomless mimosas and champagne, which is quite a steal. And when it comes to desserts, prepare to be amazed.

One of the standout features of Wicked Spoon is its slightly cozier atmosphere, making it feel more intimate than your typical buffet. The staff is friendly, adding to the overall positive experience. Make it a point to indulge in the Wicked Spoon Brunch – it's a must-visit for sure!

# BEYOND THE NEON: EXPLORING THE CITY

## Downtown Las Vegas

Downtown Las Vegas, sometimes known as "Old Las Vegas," is the heart of the city's past. It differs from the well-known Las Vegas Strip, which lies a few miles south.

Downtown Las Vegas can be neatly divided into three distinctive sections, each offering its own unique charm and attractions. Let's explore these areas:

**Fremont Street Experience** where you'll find the iconic canopy and a cluster of lively casinos. So Fremont Street Experience is the beating heart of downtown Las Vegas.

**Fremont East**: If you're seeking trendy restaurants and vibrant nightlife, this is the place to be. Locals often gather here for a weekend full of great dining and drinks.

**Arts District**: For those in search of a more artistic and laid-back vibe, the Arts District is a gem. Here, you'll discover quaint coffee shops, breweries, and upscale restaurants that cater to diverse tastes.

While Las Vegas is truly renowned for the Strip, the Fremont Street Experience offers more of that old-school vibe. This was the original strip before the Strip even existed, and many locals actually prefer this section over the Strip itself.

- Fremont Street Experience:

The Fremont Street Experience is one of Downtown Las Vegas' most recognizable landmarks. Fremont Street is divided into a pedestrian walkway and entertainment district that spans five blocks. The Viva Vision Light Show, a sizable LED light show above the street canopy, provides nightly music and visual performances.

Walking down Fremont Street is an experience everyone should have at least once in their lifetime. I've had the chance to visit a few times during the day, but my first visit at night was an entirely different adventure.

The 5-block-long overhead display is truly something else. You'll encounter live bands playing music on every corner, street performers showing off their skills, magicians pulling off incredible tricks, contortionists bending in unbelievable ways, celebrity look-alikes, and showgirls all around you.

If you don't mind a sensory overload, Fremont Street is an absolute must-visit. The nighttime lights are simply incredible, and the sheer number of people – over 150,000 at times – adds to the excitement. The casinos are bustling with slot machines, and they hold their own when it comes to payouts and hit ratios.

Honestly, I wish I had visited Fremont Street a long time ago. It's a must-see in Vegas! Just keep an eye out for pickpockets. Fortunately, there's a strong police presence to help keep things safe at night.

A Bucket List of Top Fremont Street Experiences

### The SlotZilla Zipline

SlotZilla is a thrilling zip line attraction located at the Fremont Street Experience in downtown Las Vegas. Resembling a colossal slot machine, this attraction offers two different take-off levels for an exciting adventure.

Flying over Fremont Street on SlotZilla is an absolute blast. The overall experience is truly awesome, and one of the cool features is that you can have pictures of your flight sent directly to your phone, including some great still shots. I highly recommend giving this a try if you're looking for an adrenaline-pumping adventure.

### Viva Vision Light Shows

The free light shows featuring the world's largest digital display, are an absolute must-see during your visit. These mesmerizing shows take place nightly, with a performance at the top of each hour. It's a truly magical experience that you shouldn't miss!

### Free Live Music

Fremont Street Experience hosts free live music every evening, featuring incredible performances by some of Las Vegas' most renowned musical talents. Be sure to catch the **Downtown Rocks Concert Series** too, where the Fremont Street Experience and partner casinos present the most significant concert series in all of Las Vegas, and the best part is, it's absolutely free.

## The Neon Museum

The Neon Museum will give you a nostalgic glimpse into old Las Vegas. Because it is showcasing over 200 retired signs from various casinos and businesses. During a tour of the museum's two-acre courtyard, you'll encounter massive, dazzling signs and learn about their intriguing histories. You can also enjoy the "Brilliant!" show, an incredible augmented reality experience that brings 40 neon signs back to life. Be sure to visit the gift shop for souvenirs and the visitor's center, housed within the former La Concha Hotel lobby.

While the Neon Museum opens in the late afternoon, it truly comes alive after sunset when the signs are illuminated. Nothing embodies Las Vegas more than neon signs, making this a must-visit if you crave a taste of old Vegas. They offer various tours, including the "Brilliant Experience," which I found quite enjoyable. I suggest starting with the approximately 40-minute "Guided Tour" and then exploring the "Brilliant" tour, which lasts around 35 minutes. You can purchase a combo ticket for about $45 per person. It's advisable to buy your tickets early, as they have limited spots, and many tours sell out.

For the best experience, plan your visit around sunset to witness the signs come to life as the sun sets. You'll see iconic signs like the "Stardust" and the old Hard Rock Cafe guitar sign, but there are many lesser-known signs, each with a captivating story that knowledgeable tour guides share. The "Brilliant" tour doesn't require a guide; it's more of a show, and the illusion of the signs lighting up is truly impressive. They feature great music by artists like Elvis, Frank Sinatra, and Dean Martin, adding to the magic of the signs. If you do both tours, expect to spend about two hours here.

Keep in mind that cameras aren't allowed, but you can use your cell phone for photos. Be prepared to go through a metal detector. The Neon Museum is conveniently located near downtown, just off the Las Vegas Strip at 770 Las Vegas Blvd North. It's recommended to visit at dusk or later when many of the artworks are brilliantly illuminated.

The Neon Museum's Hours of Operation are as follows:

March to April: 3:00 PM to 11:00 PM

May to August: 4:00 PM to midnight

September to October: 3:00 PM to 11:00 PM

November to February: 2:00 PM to 10:00 PM

The museum offers several packages, so if you're unsure which one suits you best, contact customer service at (702) 387-6366.

## Circa's Sportsbook

Circa offers an exceptional sports betting experience across three levels, all centered around a massive 78-million-pixel high-definition screen. What sets this sportsbook apart is not just the incredible screen but also the incredibly friendly customer service. Additionally, you can catch in-depth analysis from experts at VSiN's on-site studio, enhancing your betting experience.

One remarkable thing I observed is that people can't resist taking pictures here – the sheer excitement is palpable. At Circa Sports and at the Stadium Swim, it genuinely feels like you're right there at the game. Imagine the feeling of being at your favorite baseball park or basketball arena; that's the kind of atmosphere you'll find here.

## Happy Buddha at The California Hotel & Casino

In need of a little extra luck during your Las Vegas trip? Don't forget to give the Happy Buddha's belly a rub at The California Hotel & Casino. You'll spot this cheerful statue in the hotel's registration area. It's a fun tradition, and here's an interesting tidbit: any coins left at the statue are collected and later donated to charity. So, not only do you get a dose of good fortune, but you also contribute to a good cause by participating in this charming gesture.

# Mob Museum (National Museum of Organized Crime and Law Enforcement)

The Mob Museum is an absolutely captivating experience! It's not just about learning how the mob was connected to Las Vegas, but it delves into its origins and ongoing presence. While there's quite a bit of reading involved, they also provide information through short films. Just a heads up, there are additional paid options because the museum itself can be a bit pricey. However, these extras can be amazing supplements to your visit!

The museum opens at 9:00 AM, and it's a good idea to go as early as possible. By the time I left at 11:00 AM, there was already a line forming. After 5:00 PM, there's a discount, and the museum stays open until 9:00 PM. Your ticket (wristband) is valid until closing time, so you can take your time exploring.

It's a MUST-see attraction, and it's only a short ride from the Strip, located about two blocks from Fremont Street. Be sure to snap the classic tourist picture with 1920s and 30s mobster hats and attire available for fun photos. There's no pressure to buy a big package at the gift shop on your way out, and the prices are quite reasonable. The museum houses fascinating artifacts like a gas chamber chair, a Tommy gun, Capone's pistol, and more. Plus, the gift shop offers plenty of intriguing items. The location is in the downtown area, just a few blocks from the Fremont Street Experience.

## Berlin Wall at Main Street Station

A sizable portion of the Berlin Wall is located inside the men's restroom at Main Street Station. Ladies, don't worry, you can even ask for a security escort to see this fascinating mystery.

This undiscovered gem is nestled away in a hotel that is furnished with a ton of antiques and oddities from around the globe. You may pick up a brochure listing all the antiques spread throughout the hotel at the registration counter if you want to learn more about these fascinating relics.

## Fremont Casino

If you're a fan of craps, I highly recommend a visit to the Fremont Dice Club at Fremont Casino in downtown Las Vegas. This unique club features plaques that commemorate the names of players who have experienced impressive winning streaks at the hotel's craps tables. Additionally, you can find another collection of these plaques at Fremont's sister hotel, the nearby California Hotel & Casino.

Fremont Casino stands out as the only casino I'm aware of that uses a roll counter on its craps tables to keep a record of these memorable hot streaks for posterity.

## The Tank Pool at the Golden Nugget

The Golden Nugget's $30 million pool is truly a sight to behold. When you see it, you will realize what an incredible engineering marvel it is. One of its standout features is the massive 200,000-gallon shark tank, which you can admire from a distance or get up close to for a unique experience. However, the real highlight is taking a ride on the pool's thrilling three-story water slide. It's an adventure you won't want to miss!

## Vegas Vic

This character is a true throwback to the past, representing a bygone era of Las Vegas but remaining a recognizable figure worldwide. He's a neon sign that truly comes to life when illuminated, yet he stands as a well-preserved piece of enduring history that continues to captivate and showcase Downtown Vegas to its fullest potential even today.

Vegas Vic embodies the spirit of old-school Las Vegas and remarkably, he has managed to avoid becoming a relic in a neon graveyard. Standing tall, he's a prominent figure that's hard to miss. Although the Pioneer casino in Las Vegas has faded into history, there's still a Pioneer casino in Laughlin, NV, which is worth a visit if you happen to be in that town.

## Fremont East Entertainment District

The Fremont East Entertainment District may be relatively short in length, but it's packed with entertainment from end to end. Whether you're into ziplining, street performers, live music, diverse dining options, or shopping, you'll want to allocate a couple of hours to explore it all. This area is exclusively for pedestrians, except for a few spots where roads intersect. It's well-lit and easy to navigate, although I can't confirm the locations of public restrooms.

The Fremont East District is a hidden gem within Fremont Street, offering an array of bars, clubs, casinos, and attractions once you cross N. Las Vegas

Blvd. This area truly comes to life with its vibrant nightlife scene. While you're there, don't miss the opportunity to visit the Downtown Container Park – it's a fantastic experience.

If you're already enjoying the Fremont Street Experience, don't forget to venture across the street to the Fremont East District. It's well worth your time, and I can personally vouch for the enjoyment you'll find there.

## The Downtown Container Park

Downtown Container Park is truly a one-of-a-kind open-air venue that combines shopping, dining, and entertainment in a way you won't find anywhere else. Situated in the thriving Downtown neighborhood of Las Vegas, this innovative complex is constructed from repurposed shipping containers and locally manufactured Xtreme cubes – a unique and sustainable design.

At the park, you will be greeted by a remarkable 35-foot-tall praying mantis sculpture that shoots flames from its antennae, setting the tone for the extraordinary experience inside. Once you step in, you'll discover a whimsical world filled with exclusive boutiques, restaurants, and bars. The park also boasts a stage for presentations and live music performances, along with The Treehouse, an interactive play area featuring a 33-foot-tall slide, NEOS play system, oversized foam building blocks, and more.

It's worth noting that Downtown Container Park is open to all ages, but it transitions into a 21+ facility after 9 p.m. daily. If you're seeking a unique and unparalleled destination that sets Las Vegas apart, this is the place to be. You won't want to miss the chance to enjoy a drink while exploring this extraordinary space – and don't forget to experience the fiery art sculpture

(Praying Mantis) that welcomes you with its brilliant flames. The combination of art, boutique shops, live music, and even a play area for kids makes it a must-visit spot.

## Banger Brewing

I stumbled upon this charming little brewery tucked away in a corner of the Fremont Street Experience, and it was almost hidden by the marquee of a popular restaurant. It's one of those hidden gems that can easily go unnoticed. But let me tell you, the beer they serve here is fantastic! They offer a great variety of brews, and it's evident that the folks behind this place are passionate about what they do.

The service is not only friendly but also incredibly knowledgeable. During my visit, I opted for a sample flight, and let me tell you, it was a tough decision to pick a favorite among their beers. The Cream Ale stood out with its delightful nutty flavor, while the Coffee Kolsch was a flavorful and light option. The Jalapeño Hefeweizen struck the perfect balance of flavor without overwhelming heat. 8I especially enjoyed their El Heffe beer, which had a jalapeño hefe style and a slight kick of spiciness. The Morning Joe, packed with coffee aroma, was another highlight. They even had a few fruit-infused beers that I absolutely adored.

I was particularly pleased that I dropped by during their Happy Hour, which runs from 1-3 PM daily, offering $5 beers. Being conveniently located right on Fremont Street, it's a great spot to unwind and enjoy some quality brews.

## Old Las Vegas Mormon Fort

The Old Las Vegas Mormon Fort is a historical gem with deep roots in the city's past. Constructed by missionaries back in 1855, this fort is often referred to as the birthplace of Las Vegas. Today, it's managed by Nevada State Parks and offers visitors a chance to explore the city's history through its museum, a reconstruction of the fort, and the oldest standing building in the entire state of Nevada.

I stumbled upon this museum quite by accident, and I'm thrilled that I decided to make a stop. It's a fascinating place with both indoor and outdoor exhibits. One highlight is the oldest standing structure in Nevada, which is truly a piece of living history. The admission fee was very reasonable and well worth it, especially considering the informative 15-minute video on the fort's history and the broader history of Las Vegas.

What I appreciated most was the respectful representation of the native Paiute people for their contributions to the area. The State Park Ranger on duty was friendly and helpful, readily answering questions and even providing recommendations for other similar attractions in the vicinity.

Inside the exhibit hall, I delved into the prehistoric era, early inhabitants, and European visitors to the region, including the Spanish Jesuit parties, the Mormon immigration, farming, and the impact of railroads. It was quite intriguing to watch the short 15-minute film and explore the various exhibits, all within the comfort of an air-conditioned building. While the outdoor grounds may be of less interest, the presence of Las Vegas Creek (or its artificial representation) still flows through the fort grounds, adding to the historical ambiance. This museum is a pleasant departure from the hustle and bustle of the Strip, allowing you to discover another side of Las Vegas.

## Zak Bagans' The Haunted Museum

The Zak Bagans Museum is quite an intriguing place filled with some truly unusual and eerie items. If you're someone who is sensitive to supernatural phenomena, such as being clairvoyant, I'd strongly recommend seeking protection before entering. The museum boasts a collection of exhibits that delve into dark and unsettling territory, so it's essential to take precautions if you're prone to spiritual experiences.

Regarding admission, the General Admission package offers a unique opportunity for potential upgrades before the tour officially kicks off. One notable advantage of the general admission is that, while others are busy with the "VIP" portion, you have extra time to explore the exhibits. This can be particularly valuable since the museum can feel rushed due to the influx of visitors and the staff's efforts to stick to their allotted time slots.

During my visit, I encountered a rather chilling experience in one of the hallways. I suddenly felt a deep coldness in my legs, causing me to shiver and experience a sensation of ringing and pressure in my ears—a telltale sign for me, given my clairaudience abilities. It's worth noting that this could potentially be attributed to the air conditioning, though it was too dark to say for certain. The museum employed flashing lights for dramatic effect, and in the midst of this, I believe I saw a shadowy figure dart across the room. Even my husband, who isn't typically a believer, mentioned feeling as if someone were pinching his neck when we were alone in a room.

All in all, the experience at Zak Bagans' museum is well worth the investment, regardless of the package you choose. The staff is both humorous and knowledgeable, always willing to answer any questions you might have. I wholeheartedly recommend this experience to anyone with an interest in the paranormal, the macabre, or those who are simply familiar with the shows associated with Zak Bagans.

## Gold Spike

Gold spike is the place to go if you have a passion for gambling but aren't too keen on parting with all your money at the upscale casinos on the Strip. But if you want to go, make sure you don't mind a slightly unconventional atmosphere – one that's not all glitz and glamor. This is because Gold Spike is rather filled with plenty of smoke and the company of intriguing locals. Also, if you're looking to enjoy games like $2 Blackjack and penny slots, then I'd suggest checking out the Gold Spike.

## Where to Eat in Downtown Las Vegas

- Heart Attack Grill

Step on the scale, and if you weigh over 350 pounds, your meal is on the house. It's a unique and entertaining experience. Approach this experience with an open mind and a hearty appetite. It's a truly unique dining adventure. While the food may not be the healthiest, it's undeniably delicious, and the staff is friendly. I ordered a single burger and some onion rings. Don't count on finding any diet soda, but they do have bottled water available. Keep in mind that if you don't finish your burger, you might get a playful spanking. It's all in good fun and not painful. Just remember, you're in Las Vegas, so brace yourself for an eccentric and entertaining experience.

- Eureka! Discover American Craft

You should give Eureka a try for dining. This place serves exceptionally delicious food. When I dined there, I ordered their Mac n' Cheese balls and their wings. The Mac n' Cheese balls were absolutely fantastic with a flavorful kick. The wings were also a treat, crispy and tasting like they were homemade.

When you dine at Eureka!, you can expect not only a delectable menu of high-quality burgers and appetizers. The extensive selection of whiskeys and microbrews will also serve well to enhance your experience. Their beverage menu includes a variety of options, such as rye and bourbon. Many people prefer the single malt whiskeys while craft beer lovers love to indulge in a range of IPAs, stouts, and saisons.

- Flippin' Good Chicken, Burgers, Beer

Flipping Good is where you'll savor what might just be the best chicken sandwich you've ever had, or perhaps the absolute best! I highly recommend trying the Dirty Bird, which is a chicken sandwich with a sunny-side-up egg on top. The seasoning and rub on the chicken are absolutely fantastic. The staff is incredibly friendly, attentive, and polite, and the establishment is well-maintained and clean. If you're in the area, this is a definite must-stop for lunch or dinner. Plus, the prices are reasonable.

- Evel Pie

A treat for fans of Evel Knievel with excellent pizza.

Evel Pie is a fantastic place to enjoy a delicious slice of pizza. It has a cool, relaxed vibe, and while it's not fancy, it's clean and the food is excellent. What's even better is that kids are welcome here! The pizza is always amazing, and don't miss out on their fantastic garlic knots. The servings are generous, and the pizza is some of the best in town. Evel Pie is definitely worth a visit. They also have a special deal for cheese pizza and beer.

## Bars and Nightclubs in Downtown Las Vegas

- The Griffin Bar:

When you visit The Griffin Bar, you can expect a unique and distinct atmosphere that sets it apart from other bars in Vegas. It has a vibe that makes you feel like you're in an underground establishment, creating a one-of-a-kind setting. The bartender is friendly and knowledgeable, ready to assist you with your drink choices from their diverse selection.

Expect also, a unique contrast of elements that come together to create an interesting and appealing atmosphere. Despite being in the desert, the fireplace in the middle of the bar adds to its charm. The decor carries a vaguely Medieval theme, featuring brick walls, arches, and firepits, which provide a cozy and inviting ambiance.

The bar also features a back room where live shows often take place. These shows may require separate tickets, but even if you don't attend them, you can still enjoy the bar's ambiance, including the inviting fireplaces. It's a great place to have a memorable and different night out in Vegas. This bar is also perfect for good conversations and music.

Inspire Bar: A three-story bar that's popular with tourists, offering a lively atmosphere.

- The Laundry Room

When you visit the Laundry Room, be prepared for an amazing and unique experience. This small "speakeasy" exudes a 1920s ambiance that you'll love. It's advisable to make reservations well in advance to secure your spot because it's a popular place. The experience here is like a personal show, and it's unlike anything you'd expect in Vegas. The personalized service and attention to detail make it feel like a world apart from the typical Vegas scene.

One standout feature is the absence of loud music or flashing lights, creating a quiet and intimate atmosphere. The staff goes above and beyond to ensure you have a memorable time, making you feel genuinely welcome. If you're seeking an unconventional Vegas experience, this is the place to be.

The drinks are exceptional and highly unique, providing you with a cocktail experience that's among the best in the world. Keep in mind that opting to see a show may increase the price point, but the overall experience is well worth it.

- Therapy

The first time I dined at Therapy, it was for brunch, and the experience was fantastic. The service was excellent, and the food was delicious. I ordered the chick biscuit, while my partner tried the blackberry French toast, which he raved about, describing it as phenomenal. The restaurant has a beautiful and laid-back atmosphere, making it a great place to enjoy both great food and cocktails.

During my next visit, I tried the ceviche, penne pasta, and atomic mushroom burger. The host and server were incredibly welcoming and attentive. To complement my meal, I ordered the smoke bowl cocktail, and it was absolutely delicious.

## Parking in Downtown

Keep in mind that parking downtown typically comes with a fee, and free parking options are limited, usually available for casino Rewards members.

When parking on the street or in a public parking lot in downtown Las Vegas, you'll typically use one of the parking machines. Here's how it works:

- Input your license plate number on the machine.
- The machine will prompt you to insert your credit card.
- Choose the number of hours you plan to stay and pay accordingly.

This system helps manage parking in the area, so make sure to follow the instructions on the machine to avoid any issues. Enjoy your time exploring downtown Las Vegas.

# Vegas Beyond Gambling: Unique Experiences

## The Art District

The Arts District is a captivating neighborhood nestled between the northern end of the Las Vegas Strip and Fremont Street in the downtown area. It's a vibrant area filled with numerous breweries, antique shops, and thrift stores. If you're eager to explore this neighborhood, I recommend renting scooters from Atomic Scooters for a leisurely cruise.

Let me share some cool stops and tips for your next visit to Vegas. I personally adore this area because it exudes trendiness, eclecticism, and offers a completely different vibe compared to your typical Las Vegas experience.

One of the primary attractions of the Arts District is the abundance and diversity of unique stores. You'll discover boutique and vintage shops, antique malls, markets, thrift stores, and much more. Even if you're not on a specific shopping mission, strolling through these quirky shops and hunting for treasures or pieces of Vegas history can be a delightful change of pace.

What awaits you here? Well, there's Koolsville Tattoo, famous for its $10 tattoos in Las Vegas. If you're feeling adventurous, you might want to give it a try.

Murals

The Arts District is renowned for its exceptional street art. Sculptures and murals have become synonymous with this part of Vegas. You could easily spend an entire day wandering through its 18 blocks, constantly discovering new and captivating murals. A significant contributor to this artistic explosion is the Life is Beautiful Music and Arts Festival, which made its debut in 2013 and has been transforming downtown into a visual feast ever since.

This District is notably renowned for its impressive array of craft breweries situated along Brewery Row. Each of these establishments puts its own unique spin on crafting high-quality brews, ensuring there's something to satisfy every palate. If you can't explore them all, allow me to share a few of my personal favorites.

- Servehzah Bottle Shop and Tap Room

First up is Servehzah Bottle Shop and Tap Room. What sets this place apart is its Mexican influence on many of the beers. I highly recommend indulging in the Michelada flight, where each beer sampler is transformed into a Michelada. You'll savor fruit-infused lagers like mango, pineapple, guava, alongside the classic Mexican lager. Abel Baker, a local favorite, is an excellent starting point. At the southern end of the district is where it is. This brewery pays homage to Nevada's Atomic Testing history and boasts an impressive selection of over 30 beers on tap. The ambiance exudes a casual and inviting vibe, with the Tap Room offering an indoor-outdoor patio feel.

Neon Desert Brewing is a must-visit spot, and what's not to adore about a tap room adorned in vibrant green and pink shades? With a dozen enticing beer options on tap, the standout choice has to be the "11 Circles of Helis." Here, you get to customize your spice level on a scale from 1 to 11. This beer features a medley of ghost, Serrano, and habanero peppers. I opted for a spicy level 7 out of 11, and it delivered quite the kick. I can only imagine how wild a 9 or 10, let alone an 11, would be. But it's an experience you've got to try for yourself. It's like the one-chip challenge but with beer!

Next up is Luv-it Frozen Custard, a true Las Vegas institution that has stood the test of time for decades. It's a walk-up window offering a delightful array of Frozen Custard flavors. The crowd favorite here is the "Western Special," featuring hot caramel, hot fudge, salted pecans, and a maraschino cherry. When the desert heat hits and you're yearning for something cold and indulgent, make sure to savor this classic Las Vegas treat. Just remember to enjoy it quickly!

Step inside the Arts Factory, a transformed warehouse that serves as a vibrant creative hub. Here, you'll discover a treasure trove of creativity with over 30 small galleries and artist studios. It's an ever-evolving space that showcases rotating exhibitions from both local talents and international artists. The best part? Strolling through the maze-like hallways and admiring the art won't cost you a dime.

While you explore, be sure to visit the art shops where you can find unique jewelry and much more. And here's a little insider tip: Keep an eye out for the art vending machine. It's a whimsical feature that allows you to purchase small, curated pieces of art from local artists. The mystery of what's inside that vending machine is part of the fun. What do you think you might find in the mystery box?

Guided Tours

Exploring the Arts District and parts of downtown Las Vegas is a blast, and one fantastic way to do it is by taking a guided e-scooter tour with Atomic Scooters. You've got two options here:

First, there's the self-guided tour. You'll receive a map, and then you can explore at your own pace, discovering the funky streets and stopping at four fantastic taco joints and a dessert spot. Plus, you'll have plenty of chances to snap some fun photos along the way.

Or, if you prefer a more guided experience, you can join a small group tour led by Atomic Scooters. This tour lasts about two hours and includes gliding along the lively sidewalks, enjoying some amazing food stops, and having a blast with photo opportunities. To book either of these tours, simply head to atomicscooters.com.

Another option for seeing the best of the Arts District is to join a walking tour with Taste Buzz Tours. This tour offers a mix of sightseeing and foodie experiences. Your guide will lead you through the neighborhood's coolest streets, showing you the best murals for epic photo ops, famous wedding chapels, and hidden gems you might not discover on your own. Along the way, you'll get to savor coffee, tacos, pizza, local beers, desserts, and much more. It's a fantastic way to dive into the heart of the Arts District!

For all you pop culture and cosplay enthusiasts out there, Millennium Fandom Bar is a must-visit spot. This local bar and hangout haven is a treasure trove of memorabilia and props from your favorite cult classic movies and TV shows. Not only is the decor absolutely spot-on, but they also boast an extensive menu of pop culture-inspired cocktails that'll make any fan's heart skip a beat.

What's really cool about this place is its moody and dimly lit atmosphere, which really helps showcase all the awesome props. And yes, you can indeed wield lightsabers here! Plus, if you're decked out in cosplay, you'll even get a discount.

It's just an all-around pleasant place with friendly folks. You'll find various nerdy items adorning the walls, and part of the bar has a room where vendors sell handmade pop-culture-related goodies. It's a fantastic nerdy hangout where you can enjoy a drink and explore your favorite fandoms.

Before you venture into the Arts District, here are some handy tips to keep in mind:

**Timing**: There's no rush to go early as most places don't open until around 11 AM. Use the morning to enjoy a nice breakfast or brunch elsewhere and then make your way to the Arts District.

**Safety and Walkability**: The neighborhood is very safe during the daytime, so you can explore with peace of mind. If you're short on time and want to cover more ground, consider renting e-scooters. It's a great way to take a break from walking, especially when a typical day in Vegas involves around 20,000 steps.

**Transportation**: To reach the Arts District, you can easily take a ride-sharing service like Uber or Lyft. The cost should be around $8 to $12 if you're coming from the Strip. This can give you an estimate if you plan to take a taxi instead. Alternatively, you can hop on the Downtown Loop shuttle from the Strat Hotel. It's a free shuttle service that operates during the day.

**Ideal for Repeat Visitors**: While the Arts District is a fantastic place to explore, it might not be a top priority for first-time visitors to Vegas, especially if you have a shorter stay. However, it's perfect for those who've been to Vegas before and want to discover new areas beyond the usual attractions.

# ACCOMMODATIONS

**Luxurious Retreats: Top Hotels and Resorts**

FOUR SEASONS HOTEL LAS VEGAS

Pros:

- Non-gaming hotel with a serene atmosphere
- Luxurious rooms and suites with all the amenities
- World-class spa and fitness center
- Multiple award-winning restaurants
- Convenient location on the Las Vegas Strip

Cons:

- Can be expensive, especially during peak season
- Limited casino and entertainment options
- Resort fee not included in room rate
- Cost: Rooms start at around $500 per night, suites start at around $1,000 per night

Facilities:

- Spa and fitness center
- Multiple restaurants and bars
- Outdoor pool and lounge
- Business center
- Concierge service

BELLAGIO HOTEL & CASINO

Pros:

- Iconic hotel with a world-famous fountain show
- Luxurious rooms and suites with stunning views
- Multiple award-winning restaurants and bars

- High-energy casino and entertainment scene
- Convenient location in the heart of the Las Vegas Strip

Cons:

- Can be very crowded and noisy, especially on weekends
- Resort fee not included in room rate
- Some facilities, such as the spa and pool, can be expensive
- Cost: Rooms start at around $200 per night, suites start at around $500 per night

Facilities:

- Casino and entertainment complex
- Spa and fitness center
- Multiple restaurants and bars
- Outdoor pool and garden
- Botanical garden
- Art gallery
- Business center
- Concierge service

SKYLOFTS AT MGM GRAND

Pros:

- Ultra-luxury hotel with private access and concierge service
- Spacious lofts with all the amenities, including kitchens and balconies
- Preferred access to MGM Grand dining, entertainment, and nightclubs
- Convenient location on the Las Vegas Strip

Cons:

- Very expensive

- Resort fee not included in room rate
- Cost: Lofts start at around $1,000 per night

Facilities:

- Private access and concierge service
- Spacious lofts with all the amenities
- Preferred access to MGM Grand dining, entertainment, and nightclubs
- Outdoor pool and lounge
- Fitness center
- Business center

THE VENETIAN RESORT-PALAZZO PRESTIGE CLUB LOUNGE

Pros:

- Luxurious suites with access to the exclusive Prestige Club Lounge
- Private check-in and check-out
- Complimentary breakfast, afternoon snacks, and evening cocktails
- Priority access to restaurants and entertainment
- Convenient location on the Las Vegas Strip

Cons:

- Very expensive
- Resort fee not included in room rate
- Cost: Suites start at around $1,000 per night

Facilities:

- Prestige Club Lounge with private check-in and check-out, complimentary breakfast, afternoon snacks, and evening cocktails, and priority access to restaurants and entertainment
- Multiple restaurants and bars

- Outdoor pool and lounge
- Fitness center
- Gondola rides
- Shopping mall
- Business center
- Concierge service

## Boutique Stays: Unique Lodging Options

**The Downtowner**

Pros:

- Stylish and affordable Art Deco hotel in downtown Las Vegas
- Well-appointed rooms with modern amenities
- Public areas decorated with vintage artwork and furniture
- Convenient location to downtown attractions

Cons:

- Limited amenities, such as no pool or spa
- Can be noisy at times due to its downtown location
- Resort fee not included in room rate
- Cost: Rooms start at around $200 per night

Facilities:

- Well-appointed rooms with modern amenities
- Public areas decorated with vintage artwork and furniture
- 24-hour front desk
- Business center
- Fitness center
- Laundry facilities

The Serene Vegas Boutique Hotel

Pros:

- Intimate and relaxing hotel just off the Las Vegas Strip
- Spacious rooms with all the amenities you need for a comfortable stay
- Two outdoor pools and cabanas
- Quiet and peaceful atmosphere

Cons:

- Limited amenities, such as no casino or spa
- Can be expensive, especially during peak season
- Resort fee not included in room rate
- Cost: Rooms start at around $300 per night

Facilities:

- Spacious rooms with all the amenities you need for a comfortable stay
- Two outdoor pools and cabanas
- 24-hour front desk
- Business center
- Fitness center
- Laundry facilities

The Lexi Las Vegas

Pros:

- Fun and funky adults-only hotel on the Las Vegas Strip
- Rooms decorated in a variety of eclectic styles
- Lively pool and lounge area
- Convenient location to Strip attractions

Cons:

- Limited amenities, such as no spa
- Can be noisy and crowded at times
- Resort fee not included in room rate
- Cost: Rooms start at around $250 per night

Facilities:

- Rooms decorated in a variety of eclectic styles
- Lively pool and lounge area
- 24-hour front desk
- Business center
- Fitness center
- Laundry facilities

The Thunderbird Boutique Hotel

Pros:

- Retro-inspired hotel just off the Las Vegas Strip
- Rooms decorated in a mid-century modern style
- Public areas feature vintage artwork and furniture
- Affordable rates

Cons:

- Can be noisy at times due to its proximity to the Las Vegas Strip
- Resort fee not included in room rate
- Cost: Rooms start at around $150 per night

Facilities:

- Rooms decorated in a mid-century modern style
- Public areas feature vintage artwork and furniture
- 24-hour front desk
- Business center
- Fitness center

- Laundry facilities

## Making the Most of Your Hotel Experience

Book Directly with the Hotels: To snag great deals on Las Vegas hotels, start by booking directly through their websites. This typically offers the best rates. Avoid making phone reservations, as they may cost more.

Join Players Clubs: Sign up for players' clubs like M life for MGM properties and Total Rewards for Caesars Properties. When searching for room rates, be sure to log in with your Players Club account. Membership often comes with lower room rates.

Take Advantage of Perks: After joining players' clubs, keep an eye on your email inbox. You'll receive frequent updates on promotions and special offers. These deals can include discounted rates, so it's essential to stay in the loop.

Plan Ahead: Some promotions offer rates for stays over the next year. While you need to book promptly, these rates can be locked in for future trips. Don't forget to click the "book now" link in the emails to access these exclusive rates for club members.

Start with a Refundable Rate: When booking a hotel, opt for the refundable rate, which allows you to cancel or modify your reservation while getting your money back. This provides flexibility in case your plans change.

Regularly Check Rates: Even after booking a refundable rate, keep an eye on the hotel's website. Rates can fluctuate based on demand. Check every few days or weekly to see if prices have dropped.

Seize Last-Minute Deals: Hotels may initially set high rates, assuming a surge in visitors. However, closer to your stay, they might realize that demand is lower than expected. This is when they often slash prices. Be ready to adjust your reservation to the lower rate just a few days before your stay.

Consider Prepaid Rates: If your travel plans are solid and you're booking just a few days before your stay, explore prepaid rates. These rates are typically 10% to 20% cheaper than refundable ones and can be a great deal if you're certain about your trip.

Leverage Reward Credit Cards: When booking and paying for your hotel stay, use a rewards-earning credit card. The Chase Sapphire Reserve card, for example, earns three Ultimate Rewards points per dollar spent on travel, including hotels. These points can be highly valuable for future flights and hotel stays, providing you with up to 6% value back on your Las Vegas hotel booking.

Explore Discover it® Cash Back Card: The Discover it® Cash Back card is an excellent choice for deal hunters. It offers cash back on various purchases, helping you save on your Las Vegas expenses.

Use TopCashback for Cash Back: Consider booking through TopCashback to earn cash back on Las Vegas hotel stays. This platform has partnerships with numerous hotels, including Caesars, offering cash back on your bookings. You can still book directly with the hotels and receive any discounts they offer, while also earning cash back through TopCashback. Keep in mind that the available cash back values and partners may vary, so check their current offerings before your trip.

Leverage Affiliate Discounts: Las Vegas hotels often offer discounts for various affiliations, such as AAA, senior citizens, first responders, military personnel, and teachers. Check for affiliate discounts that you qualify for, as they can provide significant savings.

Choose Hotels with Free Parking: Some hotels in Las Vegas, like Treasure Island (TI) or The Venetian, offer free parking. If you have a car, staying at a hotel with complimentary parking can save you a substantial amount. Additionally, if you're staying at M life or Caesars properties, consider getting their credit cards, as they often provide free parking privileges.

Redeem Points for Free Rooms: If you're a member of loyalty programs like Marriott Bonvoy, Hilton Honors, or World of Hyatt, you can redeem points for free hotel stays in Las Vegas. Many affiliated hotels are located along the Strip. Keep in mind that the value of your points may vary depending on the property and its cash rates. If you're a frequent gambler, casinos may also offer comped rooms based on your play.

Consider Booking a Flight and Hotel Package: Some airlines, like Southwest Vacations, offer package deals that include both your flight and hotel stay. These packages can often provide significant savings compared to booking each separately. Be sure to explore similar offers from other airlines as well.

Opt for Midweek Stays: Las Vegas tends to be busiest on weekends when more visitors flock to the city. Room rates can be substantially higher on weekends compared to weekdays. If you're looking to save money, consider planning your visit during the week. You'll often find lower room rates and fewer crowds. Additionally, check Las Vegas convention calendars to avoid major events that can drive up prices. Be particularly cautious around events like CES (Consumer Electronics Show) and World of Concrete, as well as during holiday periods like New Year's Eve when room rates are typically higher.

Consider Off-Strip Hotels: Staying at a hotel off the Las Vegas Strip can often lead to significant savings. These hotels typically offer lower room rates, less expensive parking, and lower resort fees. Additionally, some off-Strip hotels include complimentary breakfast with your stay. Chains like Residence Inn, SpringHill Suites, Hyatt Place, and Hilton Homewood Suites are known for offering hearty free breakfast options. Keep in mind that while the Las Vegas Strip is a major attraction, staying off-Strip can provide excellent value.

Avoid Room Service and Minibar Costs: Room service and minibar items in Las Vegas hotels can be incredibly expensive. It's best to avoid ordering room service altogether, as the convenience comes with a hefty price tag. Additionally, exercise caution with minibar items, as they are often sensor-controlled. Simply moving an item can result in a charge appearing on your bill, even if you didn't consume it. To save money and avoid any disputes, it's best to refrain from touching minibar items altogether.

# KEEPING THE DICE ROLLING: GAMBLING AND GAMING

Embrace the Randomness: First, remember that slot machines are all about randomness. Even the most skilled players will face losses. It's simply the nature of the game.

No Beating the House: Let's be real—don't expect to outsmart the casinos or the slot machines. They always hold an advantage. The odds are inherently in their favor.

Superstitions and Charms: It's perfectly fine to believe in superstitions or carry lucky charms if they make you feel more at ease when playing. However, understand that they don't actually impact the game's outcome.

Independent Spins: Each spin on a slot machine is entirely independent of the one before it. So, don't assume that the outcome of one spin affects the next—it doesn't.

Quick Stops Don't Help: Rapidly stopping the reels won't alter your game's outcome. All it accomplishes is speeding up your gameplay. And let's not forget, slowing down can mean savoring those complimentary cocktails!
Set a Budget and Stick to It: Before you even start playing, establish a budget and commit to sticking to it. Ensure that you're only using money you can comfortably afford to lose. This budget will help you avoid overspending and keep your gambling in check.

Money Management Approach: To extend your playing time, consider a money management approach. One popular method is to divide your budget into separate parts. For example, if you have $200, split it into ten $20 sections. Play each $20 portion separately. If one section runs out, move on to the next. If you double your money on one section, pocket your winnings and continue with the others.

Choosing Slot Machines: Think about your slot machine choices. There are low volatility and high volatility machines. Low volatility machines pay out more frequently but offer smaller jackpots. High volatility machines can go through long dry spells before yielding larger payouts. If you prefer more frequent wins, opt for low volatility machines, like Double Diamonds, Triple Sevens, or classic pinball-themed slots.

High Volatility Machines: High volatility machines, like the popular Wheel of Fortune or Lightning Link, offer the chance for massive jackpots but require more patience and money. Be aware of their high-risk nature. Games with high multipliers often fall into this category.

Themed License Slots: Themed slots, such as those based on movies like The Wizard of Oz or Willy Wonka, are entertaining but usually have high volatility and lower payouts due to licensing costs.

Choose Higher Denomination Machines: When playing slot machines in Las Vegas, consider opting for higher denomination machines. These machines typically offer better payouts compared to their lower denomination counterparts.

One-Cent Machines: You'll come across plenty of one-cent slot machines in casinos. These are quite popular, but keep in mind that they're designed to be profitable for the casino. Consequently, the odds and payouts on one-cent machines tend to be less favorable for players.

Go for Higher Denominations: If your budget allows, aim to play on machines with higher denominations, like five-dollar or even twenty-five-dollar machines. These higher denomination games often have more generous payouts, increasing your chances of winning.

Multi-Denomination Slots: Some machines allow you to choose from various denominations. In such cases, it's advisable to select the highest denomination that comfortably fits within your budget. This strategy enhances your odds of securing better payouts.

Keep an Eye Out for Must-Hit Progressives: In your quest for winning in Las Vegas, it's a good idea to be on the lookout for must-hit progressive slot machines. These machines can offer fantastic opportunities for a big win, although it's important to note that as more people become aware of them, such opportunities are becoming rarer.

Example: Thunder Cash: Let's take "Thunder Cash" as an example. If you come across this machine, and it's close to reaching a major or minor payout, it might be a smart move to give it a try. The potential for a significant win could be just around the corner.

A Quick Note on Graphic Displays: Be cautious when it comes to visual elements like pots in the middle of a game, such as in "Dancing Drums." Sometimes, even if the pot looks full, it doesn't necessarily increase your odds of winning. Always remember that the odds are typically stacked against the player.

Bet Enough for Jackpots: When playing progressive slot machines, make sure you're betting an amount that qualifies you for potential jackpots. Some games may offer subpar payouts if you're not eligible for the jackpot. So, bet smart and keep your eyes open for those promising opportunities to maximize your chances of winning in Las Vegas. Good luck, and may you hit the jackpot!

Debunking a Myth: Player's Cards Don't Affect Your Odds: Let's clear up a common misconception right off the bat. Using your player's card when you're at the slots or tables in Las Vegas doesn't affect your odds of winning at all. Your chances of hitting the jackpot remain the same whether you use the card or not.

Player's Cards = Comps and Incentives: What using your player's card does is open the door to a world of benefits. Casinos want to keep you engaged and playing, so they offer you comps—complimentary rewards. These can range from free rooms and meals to show tickets and more.

Don't Leave Money on the Table: By not using your player's card, you're essentially leaving money on the table. These comps can add up and make your overall Las Vegas experience even more enjoyable. So, don't buy into the myth that using your player's card reduces your odds. Instead, swipe that card and enjoy the perks that come with it. It's a win-win!

Know When to Cash Out and Have Fun: When you're playing slots in a casino, it's essential to know when to call it quits, especially if your goal is to come out ahead. The truth is, the longer you keep spinning those reels, the higher the chances that the casino will get its hands on your hard-earned money.

Big Wins Deserve Celebration, Not Reinvestment: If you happen to hit a significant jackpot or a substantial win, resist the urge to keep playing in hopes of winning more. It's tempting, but it can also be a costly mistake.

Instead, take your winnings and enjoy the fact that you've already had a great win.

Remember the Most Important Part—Have Fun: Above all else, remember that the primary purpose of playing slots in a casino is to have a good time. While it's nice to come out ahead, the real jackpot is the fun and excitement you experience along the way. So, stay smart with your money, and most importantly, have a blast!

# EXPLORING THE ARTS AND CULTURE SCENE

## Galleries and Museums: A Cultural Perspective

### DISCOVERY Children's Museum Las Vegas

**Admissions**

**Locals with a valid Nevada ID, it's $13.50 per person. For out-of-towners, it's $16.00. And here's a great deal – if you have an EBT, SNAP, or WIC card, you can get in for just $3.00 per ticket.**

**HOURS: Closed: Monday. Sunday: 12-5 pm. Tuesday to Saturday; 10 am - 5 pm.**

If you're a family visiting Las Vegas with kids between the ages of 2 and 10. DISCOVERY Children's Museum is a nonprofit, educational wonderland designed just for kids.

With three floors filled with interactive exhibits and activities, your children will have a blast while learning through play. Older kids can freely explore, and parents can relax knowing the staff is excellent at keeping an eye out for any wandering little ones.

Since there's no restaurant on-site, consider bringing your own food for a picnic. They even allow reentry if you let them know. Plus, they validate parking, so you won't have to worry about that.

### Las Vegas Natural History Museum

This museum promises a journey through time and nature like no other. It will take you on a journey through the captivating realm of dinosaurs to the fascinating wildlife of Nevada. The highlight for many visitors is the awe-inspiring dinosaur exhibit, where these ancient giants come to life in a truly remarkable display. Their size and sounds are sure to leave you amazed.

Beyond dinosaurs, the museum boasts an array of diverse exhibits. Embark on a virtual expedition through the "Treasures of Egypt,". You can also immerse yourself in the vibrant "Marine Life Gallery," or wander through the captivating "African Savanna Gallery."

This museum is a perfect family-friendly adventure, offering an educational and entertaining experience for kids and adults alike. The exhibits offer a glimpse into different corners of the world, making it an exciting and enriching outing.

**Location: 900 Las Vegas Blvd N, Las Vegas, NV 89101-1112**

**Neighborhood: Downtown**

**Hours of Operation:**

**Wednesday to Monday: 9 am–4 pm**

**Closed on Tuesdays**

**Ticket Prices: Range from US$6–14, making it an affordable and valuable experience.**

## The Atomic Museum

Venture beyond the glitz and glamor of the Las Vegas Strip to discover the Atomic Museum. It is a unique institution dedicated to documenting the history of nuclear testing at the Nevada Test Site in the Mojave Desert. It is located at 755 E Flamingo Rd, Las Vegas, NV 89119-7363 in the Paradise neighborhood. I love it because it offers a distinctive perspective on a pivotal period in history.

The Atomic Museum delves into the development of nuclear weapons, focusing on the Nevada Test Site's role in this complex narrative. While it primarily covers the Cold War era, it also addresses contemporary issues like the containment of radioactive waste. This museum has been able to seamlessly blend science, history, politics, and popular culture into a coherent and engaging narrative, all without resorting to jingoism.

While the $24 admission fee might be slightly higher than some other attractions, the opportunity to explore this unique facet of history is well worth it. You'll find yourself away from the hustle and bustle, immersed in a thought-provoking environment.

Despite its small size, the museum is a rich and immersive experience. With three rooms housing exhibits, two shows, and a gift shop, there's much to explore. One of the shows is a sensory experience that allows you to feel the earth shake and the wind blow, adding a tangible dimension to the historical narrative. As a plus, the museum features a photography exhibit and an exploration of the social effects of the Cold War.

Hours of Operation:

**Wednesday to Monday: 9 am–5 pm**

**Closed on Tuesdays**

## Springs Preserve in Las Vegas

Address: 333 S Valley View Blvd, Las Vegas, NV 89107-4372

Admission Fees:

Adults: $18.95

Seniors (65+): $17.05

Children (5-17): $10.95

Children 4 and under: Free

Nevada residents receive discounted rates.

Admission to the Nevada State Museum is included with paid admission to Springs Preserve.

Family Passes offering FREE admission to Springs Preserve can be checked out at all Las Vegas-Clark County Library branches. Each Family Pass allows up to six people entry during a single visit to the Springs Preserve.

Springs Preserve is a sprawling 180-acre cultural institution with a mission to honor the vibrant history of Las Vegas. The preserve also serves as a facility promoting a sustainable future. This remarkable site boasts a wide range of attractions. You will find museums, galleries, and outdoor concerts. There are also events, vibrant botanical gardens, and an interpretive trail system winding through a picturesque wetland habitat.

It has been designated on the National Register of Historic Places since 1978. So you know that Springs Preserve holds the distinction of being the birthplace of Las Vegas. It stands as one of the most culturally and biologically diverse resources in Southern Nevada. Here, you'll not only immerse yourself in the history of Las Vegas but also explore the area's unique natural environment.

If you're a history enthusiast and enjoy walking, you'll find Springs Preserve to be a treasure trove of activities. The admission fee offers incredible value, granting access to tours, walking paths, museums, and much more. The site provides hours of entertainment, making it an excellent choice for a day of exploration.

While Springs Preserve offers an abundance of enjoyable outdoor sites and activities, it's advisable to visit during the fall or winter. Las Vegas summers can be scorching and drain your energy quickly, especially when spending extended periods outdoors.

*Meow Wolf's Omega Mart*

**Location: AREA15, Las Vegas, Nevada**

**General Admission: $49**

**Children, Seniors, Military: $45**

Local Discounts Apply

(Note: Entrance to AREA15 itself is free with a ticket, but there is a separate admission fee for Omega Mart. Many items within Omega Mart can be purchased both in-store and online.)

Meow Wolf's Omega Mart is located within AREA15 in Las Vegas. It is an immersive and interactive art experience that defies easy description. When you enter AREA15, it resembles a large mall with various restaurants and game rooms. However, the main attraction is Omega Mart, which is well worth the admission price for the approximately three-hour adventure it provides.

Omega Mart is designed to resemble a surreal grocery store filled with bizarre and unconventional items. For instance, you might encounter products like "P-2000 cracker spackle" that, upon closer inspection, turn out to be real peanut butter. Many of the products you encounter inside the store are actually available for purchase, both on-site and online.

Behind the facade of the grocery store lies a captivating mystery. Make sure you explore the store and progress through your "employee training," you'll gradually uncover the secret behind the enigmatic "S" that appears in all of Omega Mart's products. This narrative journey involves elements of intrigue, death, and a missing child. While it can be a bit challenging to follow the story while you're engrossed in the visual and tactile wonders around you, it adds depth to the experience.

Omega Mart is a labyrinthine world filled with interactive displays, rooms, lights, and textures. While exploring, you'll find plenty to engage with. You will find out that it is  easy to spend a significant amount of time discovering the hidden wonders within.

It's important to note that Meow Wolf's Omega Mart can be highly stimulating for some visitors. The experience includes a multitude of lights, sounds, textures, tight spaces, and a bustling atmosphere. It's a unique, alcohol-free adventure that can be enjoyed by visitors of all ages.

Before you leave, make sure to check out the gift shop. The shop offers many unique and artistic souvenirs.

## The Punk Rock Museum

**Location: 1422 Western Ave., Las Vegas, NV 89102**
**Hours; Weekdays :12:00 PM – 8:00 PM**
**Weekends: 10:00 AM – 8:00 PM**
The Punk Rock Museum will take you on  a comprehensive journey through the history of punk rock, from its roots to the present day. This unique

museum displays lovely exhibits. The knowledgeable tour guides often have firsthand experience in the music industry.

The museum collection includes punk rock memorabilia. The best part is the musicians' outfits, instruments, and artifacts. You'll find items related to a wide range of punk rock artists and bands, from well-known figures to niche and underground acts.

Each era of punk rock is thoughtfully presented with informative contextual information, quotes from artists and critics, and more. This will provide you with a deeper understanding of the evolution of punk music and its cultural significance.

The museum even features an on-site bar where visitors can enjoy a great happy hour from 7-9 pm. The signature shot, known as the "gut punch," is a noteworthy favorite among patrons.

Visitors appreciate the convenience of free parking. It is accessible for those exploring the museum and the nearby arts district.

My favorite feature is the jam room. In this room, you get to play actual guitars and basses used by famous punk rockers.

## Illuminarium Las Vegas

Illuminarium Las Vegas offers a unique experience where you can embark on adventures like an African safari, explore the depths of space, and even enjoy cocktails in a Tokyo night market. It's a place where you can immerse yourself in extraordinary experiences that range from the wonders of nature to cultural moments using cutting-edge technology like 4K interactive projection, 360° audio, floor vibrations, and scent systems. Located at 3246 W Desert Inn Rd, Las Vegas, NV 89102-8431, Illuminarium allows you to experience cinematic immersion like never before.

During the Africa Wild show, which typically lasts about 40 minutes, the screens change every five minutes to showcase new and exciting scenes. You'll feel vibrations in the room during thunderstorms or when animals are in action, and there's even a pleasant, clean floral garden scent in the air. The venue is highly accessible for those with mobility challenges, providing comfortable seating throughout. Parking is also hassle-free, especially if you arrive during less busy times, such as Sunday morning when it was quiet.

If you opt for the VIP ticket, you'll receive a $10 voucher that you can use at the Lumin Cafe. Some visitors have found the food options, like sliders with fries, to be quite satisfying, making the voucher worthwhile. Overall, it's an enjoyable experience, and you're considering returning to explore their space-themed presentation.

# PRACTICAL TIPS FOR YOUR LAS VEGAS TRIP

## Navigating the City: Transportation and Getting Around

The Deuce

The Deuce operates around the clock, 24 hours a day, starting from the South Strip Transit Terminal and making its way along the Vegas Strip with numerous stops along the resort corridor. It continues on to the Fremont Street Experience in Downtown Las Vegas and the Las Vegas Premium Outlets South.

Deuce on the Strip is your go-to mode of transportation if you're staying at or visiting any of the hotels and casinos along the famous Las Vegas Strip. You'll find convenient stops roughly every quarter mile in both directions, clearly marked with signs or bus shelters.

Compared to taxis, Las Vegas buses are a more accessible option as they can pick up passengers directly from the street. The RTC Transit system boasts 51 routes, and if you plan to spend most of your time on the Strip, the San Francisco-style double-decker Deuce is your best bet. It can accommodate up to 97 passengers, offers air-conditioning, and a roomy interior. The journey begins at the southern terminal near the Harry Reid International Airport and concludes at a terminal close to Fremont Street. Of course, you can also explore more of Las Vegas by hopping on any of the other 37 buses.

For the most up-to-date information on bus arrival times, you have several options:

Utilize the rideRTC mobile app.

Send a text with "RideRTC" and your bus stop number to 41411.

Give them a call at 702-228-RIDE (7433).

Apart from its extensive coverage of the hotels and casinos along the famous Las Vegas Resort Corridor, the Deuce on the Strip offers routes that extend both north and south, operating 24 hours a day.

Heading south, the Deuce stops at key locations like the iconic Welcome to Las Vegas Sign, the Las Vegas South Premium Outlets, and the South Strip Transit Terminal.

For those traveling northbound, the Deuce route takes you all the way to the vibrant Fremont Street Experience located in Downtown Las Vegas.

If your destination includes the Las Vegas North Premium Outlets or the Symphony Park area, you'll want to catch Routes 401 for convenient access.

## The Downtown Loop

The Downtown Loop is a convenient and free shuttle service that connects you to various exciting attractions in downtown Las Vegas. Here are some of its key stops:

Bonneville Transit Center - First Street, South of Bonneville Avenue

The Arts District - Art Way and Boulder Avenue

Arts District South - Main Street, between California and Colorado avenues

Brewery Row - 1500 Block of Main Street between Utah and Wyoming avenues

Pawn Plaza - Las Vegas Boulevard, South of Garces Avenue

Fremont East Entertainment District - Sixth Street, North of Fremont Street

Mob Museum - Stewart Avenue, West of Third Street

Fremont Street Experience - Normally Main Street just South of Fremont Street, but temporarily relocated to Main Street just north of Ogden Avenue due to construction

Las Vegas North Premium Outlets - South Grand Central Parkway, between Nautica and Tommy Hilfiger Kids

Symphony Park - Promenade Place, South of Symphony Park Avenue

The Strat hotel-casino - 2000 S. Las Vegas Blvd., in the taxi and rideshare pickup area at the rear of the property

Circa hotel-casino - First Street, North of Ogden Avenue (closed Dec. 7-11 due to construction)

(CURRENTLY UNAVAILABLE) City Hall - 495 S. Main St., South of First Street

The Downtown Loop operates from 11 a.m. to 6 p.m. on Sundays through Thursdays and from 3 p.m. to 10 p.m. on Fridays and Saturdays. During First Friday events, there's a special route running from the City Hall Garage to the 18b Arts District. The shuttle runs continuously during its operating hours, and you can track its location in real-time using the GoVegas App.

To access the Downtown Loop, you can take The Deuce bus line, which stops at various locations, including the Mob Museum, Bonneville Transit Center, and The STRAT. This provides a convenient way to connect to or exit from the Downtown Loop and return to the Las Vegas Strip.

## The Monorail

The Las Vegas Monorail is a convenient automated mass transit system spanning 3.9 miles (6.3 km) that runs alongside the famous Las Vegas Strip. It primarily serves the unincorporated communities of Paradise and Winchester, not venturing into the city of Las Vegas itself.

This monorail system features seven stations, making it easy to access key destinations:

- MGM Grand

- Bally's / Paris
- Flamingo
- Harrah's / The LINQ
- Las Vegas Convention Center
- Westgate Las Vegas
- SAHARA Las Vegas

The monorail operates daily, starting around 7:00 AM and continuing until midnight, with extended service hours on weekends and during special events. Trains arrive at each station every 4-8 minutes, ensuring efficient transportation.

Ticket fares may vary based on the number of rides you purchase, and discounts are available for seniors, children, and military personnel. For those who plan to use the monorail extensively, unlimited ride passes are also available for purchase, providing cost-effective travel options.

## Staying Safe and Healthy in Las Vegas

When you're here in Vegas, whether it's your first or hundredth time, there are some things you should really keep an eye out for. Vegas is constantly changing, and there's always a new scam or something trying to take advantage of you as a visitor. So, here are some tips to ensure you have a safe and fantastic experience in Vegas – just things to be mindful of.

First, it's no secret that there's a significant homeless population in Vegas, and you'll notice this during your visit. Most of them are harmless, often just sleeping or holding signs asking for money. However, there are some who may appear to be struggling with mental health or substance abuse issues. In such situations, it's crucial to be aware of your surroundings, trust your instincts, and if you ever feel unsafe, don't hesitate to seek refuge in a casino. Additionally, consider donating food to those in need – it's something we've found is genuinely appreciated.

Here's a pro tip to avoid rookie mistakes when booking your Las Vegas trip: steer clear of online packages through platforms like Expedia or Kayak. Instead, consider booking directly with the hotel. Often, hotels offer special deals and discounts on their own websites that you won't find elsewhere. Plus, if you encounter any issues or need assistance during your stay, the hotel staff is more equipped to help you directly. When you book directly, you're not just a guest; you're a valued customer, and the hotel will do its best to ensure you have a fantastic experience because they want to earn your loyalty and future business.

When you visit the popular 'Welcome to Fabulous Las Vegas Sign', you'll find many people waiting in a long line to take pictures. To avoid the crowd, consider coming to the side where you can still capture the sign in your photos. But if you prefer that perfect straight-on shot, it's advisable to arrive early. As the saying goes, the early bird catches the worm, and given the late-night atmosphere of Vegas, getting up early might be a good strategy to get your desired shots without the crowds.

When you stroll down Las Vegas Boulevard, you'll encounter numerous individuals vying for your attention and money. There are showgirls, people dressed as various characters, and even those who may try to put a bracelet on your wrist or hand you a CD. These folks are very much a part of the Vegas experience, and this is how they earn their living. If you're not interested in a photo or what they're selling, a polite decline and continuing on your way will do the trick. However, if you do want a photo, go for it – after all, it's Vegas! Just keep in mind that they work for tips, and they typically expect around a $20 tip on average. I've seen them get quite upset when people take photos without tipping as they anticipate.

If you want to be well-prepared, snap a photo of your parking spot, especially if you're driving in from a neighboring state or renting a car. This can be really helpful because parking structures in Vegas can get quite confusing. Having that photo will ensure you don't get lost and will make you a savvy tourist.

Inside the hotels and resorts, you'll come across friendly individuals who might approach you, asking if you'd like to pick up your show tickets or if you've received your welcome package. It's important to understand that these folks are simply trying to earn a living. However, a word of caution – the welcome gift often comes with an invitation to attend a timeshare presentation. So, if you're genuinely interested in show tickets, that's great, but if not, a polite decline will suffice, and you can continue on your way.

Avoid making the rookie mistake of exposing yourself to the sun without protection. You can protect your skin, scalp, and eyes by using an umbrella. Opt for a white umbrella, as it will reflect the sun away from both the umbrella and your skin.
Even if you're visiting Las Vegas during the winter, don't underestimate the power of the sun. The desert sun can be surprisingly intense year-round, so it's crucial to protect yourself. Be sure to apply sunscreen generously all

over your skin to prevent sunburn and skin damage. Protecting yourself from the sun is an essential part of staying comfortable and healthy during your Las Vegas trip.

Las Vegas experiences strong winds throughout the year, and with the desert terrain, dust and sand can be easily blown into your eyes. Even if you don't wear contact lenses, it's a good idea to carry some saline solution with you to rinse your eyes if needed. This simple precaution can help you avoid discomfort and ensure a more enjoyable trip without the annoyance of sandy eyes.

Another valuable tip for your visit to Vegas is to ensure you stay hydrated. Head to the Las Vegas Strip and look for your nearest ABC Stores, which you'll find scattered throughout the strip, typically around five of them. If you're on Fremont Street, make your way to the ABC store near the Plaza end of Fremont Street. Here, you can grab bottles of water for just two dollars, among other options. If you can't locate an ABC Store, CVS or Walgreens are also good alternatives for staying hydrated.

If your hotel room has a refrigerator with a small freezer, a great tip, especially for the hot summer months, is to freeze a bottle of water. You can purchase affordable water bottles, as we mentioned earlier, or consider buying a case of water from Walmart or Target. Once you have a frozen water bottle, place it in one of the grocery bags you packed in your luggage to prevent any condensation from getting on your purse or backpack. This way, you'll have a refreshing cold drink to keep you cool during your Vegas adventures.

Another important tip is to avoid buying water or beer from individuals selling them from coolers on the street. Not only is this practice illegal, but you also can't be certain about the quality or source of the water or beverages they're offering. No matter how thirsty you may be, it's crucial not to make the rookie mistake of purchasing random water or beer from street vendors on the Strip or Fremont Street. Your health and safety should always come first.

It's essential to establish a budget for gambling during your trip. This way, you can enjoy your time in Las Vegas without any regrets once you return home. Now, let's move on to the next common rookie mistake that many people make while visiting Las Vegas.

Getting a player's card might seem like common sense, but it's crucial not to overlook this tip. Your player's card can unlock various perks, such as complimentary hotel stays, free meals, and more. Even at new places like Resorts World, you can score benefits like free parking. So, be sure to obtain a player's card at every establishment you visit and use it in the slot machines to accumulate points. It's a rookie mistake to miss out on these potential rewards.

 Las Vegas can be pricey, so it's wise to check out the happy hours offered at many hotels, bars, and restaurants. During happy hours, you can often find discounted food items, sometimes even at half the regular price. This way, you can sample a variety of dishes without breaking the bank on a full meal. It's a savvy move to make the most of your dining experience in Las Vegas without splurging unnecessarily.

Another essential tip is to be mindful of your valuables. Keep them securely close to your body, such as in the front of your purse or with your bag strapped across the front of your body. Avoid carrying a wallet or phone in your back pocket, and be cautious about leaving your phone in a place where someone could easily snatch it, like at a bar or near a slot machine. In fact, I once had to confront someone who attempted to walk off with my phone.

It's also a good practice to use the safe in your hotel room and avoid carrying all your cash with you. Before leaving your room, double-check that the door is securely closed and locked to ensure peace of mind during your stay.

If you're renting a car or driving in Las Vegas, it's important to be prepared for what can feel like the wild west of driving. The roads here see a mix of driving styles, so it's wise to adopt a defensive driving approach and stay alert at all times.

Regrettably, Las Vegas is known as a hotspot for sex trafficking. To ensure your safety, consider using the buddy system whenever possible. Stay vigilant of your surroundings and try to avoid quiet, less populated areas, especially at night. Always trust your instincts – if something doesn't feel right, take action. Thankfully, there are security guards scattered around, so don't hesitate to report any suspicious or concerning activities or individuals for your peace of mind and the safety of others.

Keep an eye out for unexpected extra charges during your stay in Las Vegas. These can include fees that appear on your bill for items like water, even if you didn't order it. Additionally, be cautious of covert fees that may be passed on to you, such as casino rent fees.

When it comes to drink specials like two-for-one deals, be vigilant. Sometimes, what seems like a special offer may not be as good as it appears. For example, a bar might offer a two-for-one deal, but one of the drinks is priced at nine dollars for a single can of Miller Lite. It's essential to evaluate these deals to ensure they're truly advantageous.

You'll likely encounter club promoters, dance, or strip club promoters who make enticing offers. However, be aware that these deals may come with hidden additional fees. Don't hesitate to ask questions to clarify the terms before committing to anything. Enjoy your trip and remember that you have the right to question and understand any charges on your bill.

Furthermore, be aware that you don't always have to pay the CNF tax. Check your bill before settling it, whether you've dined at a restaurant or had drinks at a bar. Some establishments in Las Vegas may include a CNF tax, which stands for Concession and Franchise Fee, on the bill. This is actually a discretionary tax, and if you see it on your bill, you can request your server to remove it without any hassle. Not all bars in Las Vegas impose this tax, but it's a good practice to check your bill for any unexpected charges.

# WRAPPING UP YOUR LAS VEGAS ADVENTURE

## One-Day Thrill-Seeker Itinerary on the Las Vegas Strip

- Morning:

**Breakfast at HEXX Kitchen + Bar (Alexxa's Las Vegas, 3655 S Las Vegas Blvd, Las Vegas, NV 89109, United States)**: Start your day with a delicious breakfast at HEXX, located at Paris Las Vegas. Enjoy a variety of breakfast options with a view of the Bellagio Fountains.

**Bellagio Conservatory & Botanical Gardens, 3600 S Las Vegas Blvd, Las Vegas, NV 89109, United States (0.9 miles away)**: After breakfast, take a short walk to the Bellagio Hotel. Explore the breathtaking Conservatory and Botanical Gardens. Here you will see seasonal displays of flowers and plants.

Don't miss the iconic Bellagio Fountains show, which takes place right in front of the hotel. Check the show schedule for the next performance.

**Explore the Strip**: Take a walk along the Las Vegas Strip. Marvel at the architecture, watch street performers, and soak in the lively atmosphere. Be sure to visit landmarks like The Venetian, Caesars Palace, and The Mirage.

- Lunch:

**Lunch at In-N-Out Burger, 3545 S Las Vegas Blvd Suite L24, Las Vegas, NV 89109, United States ( 0.6 miles away)**: For a budget-friendly meal, grab lunch at In-N-Out Burger, located near The Linq Promenade. Try their classic burgers, fries, and shakes.

- Afternoon:

High Roller Observation Wheel: Head to The LINQ Promenade and take a ride on the High Roller, the world's tallest observation wheel. Enjoy breathtaking views of the city.

Explore The LINQ Promenade's shops, restaurants, and entertainment options. Don't forget to visit the Polaroid Fotobar for unique photo souvenirs.

- Evening:

**Dinner at Gordon Ramsay Hell's Kitchen, 3570 Las Vegas Blvd S, Las Vegas, NV 89109, United States:** Dine at Gordon Ramsay Hell's Kitchen, located at Caesars Palace. Make sure to order a gourmet meal inspired by the TV show.

**Mirage Volcano (The Mirage, 3400 S Las Vegas Blvd, Las Vegas, NV 89109, United States)**: Witness the eruption of the Mirage Volcano, a free spectacle that takes place in front of The Mirage hotel. Check the schedule for showtimes.

- Late Night:

**Nightlife at The Cosmopolitan (The Cosmopolitan of Las Vegas, 3708 Las Vegas Blvd S, Las Vegas, NV 89109, United States)**: Enjoy the vibrant nightlife scene at The Cosmopolitan of Las Vegas. Visit bars and lounges like The Chandelier and Marquee Nightclub.

- Transportation Options:

The Deuce bus offers reasonably priced all-day passes and is a good option for getting about Downtown and the Strip.

The majority of the attractions in The Strip are accessible by foot.

Use ride-sharing services like Uber or Lyft for price and convenience.

The Las Vegas Monorail offers speedy travel along the eastern side of the Strip when necessary.

One-Day Thrill-Seeker Itinerary on the Las Vegas Strip with Affordable Dining

## One-Day Itinerary for Exploring Downtown Las Vegas

- Morning:

**Breakfast at Eat (Eat., 707 Carson Ave, Las Vegas, NV 89101, United States):** Start your day with a delicious breakfast at "Eat," a popular spot known for its tasty dishes and welcoming atmosphere. Try their famous "Huevos Motuleños" or classic pancakes.

**Fremont Street Experience (Fremont Street Experience, E Fremont St, Las Vegas, NV 89101, United States):** Stroll down to the Fremont Street Experience, a pedestrian mall known for its dazzling LED canopy, street performers, and a lively atmosphere. Explore the unique shops and casinos in the area.

- Late Morning:

**The Mob Museum (The Mob Museum, 300 Stewart Ave, Las Vegas, NV 89101, United States):** Visit The Mob Museum, an engaging attraction that tells about the history of organized crime in America. Learn about law enforcement's battle against the mob and explore interactive exhibits.

- Lunch:

**Lunch at Le Thai (Le Thai, 523 Fremont St, Las Vegas, NV 89101, United States):** Head to Le Thai for lunch, a local favorite famous for its delicious Thai dishes. Don't miss the mouthwatering "Waterfall Beef."

- Afternoon:

**Neon Boneyard (The Neon Museum Las Vegas, 770 Las Vegas Blvd N, Las Vegas, NV 89101, United States):** learn about Las Vegas's neon history at the Neon Boneyard. This outdoor museum showcases vintage neon signs from famous casinos and hotels. Guided tours provide fascinating insights.

- Late Afternoon:

**Container Park (Downtown Container Park, 707 E Fremont St, Las Vegas, NV 89101, United States):** Walk over to Downtown Container Park, an open-air shopping center made of shipping containers. Explore boutique shops, grab a coffee, or an ice cream and enjoy the unique atmosphere.

- Early Evening:

**Dinner at Carson Kitchen (Carson Kitchen, 124 S 6th St #100, Las Vegas, NV 89101, United States):** Savor dinner at Carson Kitchen, it is a trendy restaurant with a menu full of creative and delectable small plates. The bacon jam and crispy chicken skins are my favorites.

- Nightlife:

Spend your evening exploring the vibrant nightlife of Fremont Street. Enjoy live music, street performances, and the famous SlotZilla Zip Line, which takes you flying high above the crowds.

Visit some of the unique cocktail bars downtown, such as "The Laundry Room" or "Velveteen Rabbit," famous for their exquisite craft cocktails.

End your night in the lively Fremont East Entertainment District. This district is known for its bars, clubs, and a vibrant nightlife scene.

## Five-Day Las Vegas Adventure Itinerary

- DAY 1

MORNING

Commence your day with a delectable breakfast at Hell's Kitchen within Caesars Palace. Following breakfast, venture to the renowned Las Vegas

Strip, where you can take a leisurely stroll to admire the opulent hotels and casinos. Don't forget to marvel at the iconic Bellagio Fountains and the Eiffel Tower replica at Paris Las Vegas.

AFTERNOON

For your midday meal, relish a mouthwatering burger at Gordon Ramsay Steak, conveniently located in Paris Las Vegas. After lunch, immerse yourself in the Fremont Street Experience in downtown Las Vegas, where you can soak in the lively ambiance, witness captivating street performers, and enjoy live music. Feel free to try your luck at one of the numerous casinos in the area.

EVENING

Experience a gastronomic delight at Le Cirque, within Bellagio, for your dinner. Subsequently, make your way to the Peppermill Fireside Lounge for a distinctive retro experience. Unwind in this cozy atmosphere, complete with neon lights and a welcoming fire pit, while sipping on cocktails.

BEDTIME

- DAY 2

Natural Wonders and Thrilling Adventures

MORNING

Start early and embark on a full-day tour to the Grand Canyon West Rim. You will be captivated by the awe-inspiring vistas and have the opportunity to walk on the famous Grand Canyon Skywalk. Enjoy a picnic lunch amidst the canyon's splendor before returning to Las Vegas.

AFTERNOON

Upon returning from the Grand Canyon, take a moment to relax at Mizumi, located within Wynn Las Vegas. Indulge in a delectable Japanese meal in a serene setting. In the afternoon, elevate your experience with a helicopter flight over the Las Vegas Strip, offering a unique perspective of the city.

EVENING

For your evening meal, savor the flavors of Italy at Lago by Julian Serrano, situated in Bellagio. Following dinner, explore the vibrant nightlife of Las Vegas by visiting one of the many bars and lounges along the Strip. Conclude the evening with a visit to a renowned nightclub like Omnia or XS.

BEDTIME

- DAY 3

Culinary Delights and Outdoor Adventures

MORNING

Commence your day with a hearty breakfast at Hash House A Go Go, located within The LINQ Hotel. Afterward, venture beyond Las Vegas to explore the captivating Valley of Fire State Park, known for its striking red rock formations and scenic hiking trails.

AFTERNOON

Indulge in a delectable lunch at Echo & Rig, situated in Tivoli Village, where you can relish succulent steaks or fresh seafood. After lunch, pay a visit to the Hoover Dam and partake in a guided tour to learn about its rich history and remarkable engineering.

EVENING

Dine on Greek cuisine at Estiatorio Milos, nestled within The Cosmopolitan, for your evening repast. Following dinner, enjoy an entertaining live performance or comedy show at one of the many entertainment venues in Las Vegas.

BEDTIME

- DAY 4

Cultural Exploration and Fine Dining

MORNING

Start your day with a visit to the Neon Museum, an institution showcasing a collection of vintage Las Vegas signs. Afterward, take a leisurely stroll through the Arts District, where you can explore local art galleries and boutiques.

AFTERNOON

For lunch, head to Carson Kitchen, located in Downtown Las Vegas. Savor a creative and flavorful meal within its trendy ambiance. After lunch, immerse yourself in the history of organized crime in Las Vegas at the Mob Museum.

EVENING

Indulge in a luxurious dining experience at Joël Robuchon, situated in MGM Grand, for your evening dinner. Subsequently, catch a live performance or concert at renowned Las Vegas venues like the Colosseum at Caesars Palace or the Park Theater.

BEDTIME

DAY 5

Farewell to Las Vegas

MORNING

Kickstart your day with a visit to the High Roller at The LINQ, where you can relish panoramic views of Las Vegas from the world's tallest observation wheel. Following your ride, enjoy a delightful breakfast at Mon Ami Gabi, nestled within Paris Las Vegas.

AFTERNOON

For your midday meal, make your way to Bacchanal Buffet, located in Caesars Palace. Here, you can indulge in a wide array of international cuisines, savoring flavors from different cultures. After lunch, take a tranquil stroll through the botanical gardens at the Bellagio.

EVENING

For your final dinner in Las Vegas, savor the culinary creations of Chef Nobu at Nobu, situated in Caesars Palace. Subsequently, relish a show or performance at one of the city's renowned theaters, such as the Colosseum at Caesars Palace or the Zappos Theater at Planet Hollywood.

BEDTIME

# CONCLUSION

Lets wrap up this journey through the dazzling desert oasis of Las Vegas. However, it's essential to acknowledge one undeniable truth: Las Vegas is an absolute treasure trove of activities and experiences. While this guidebook aimed to give you a taste of the city's magic, please remember that Las Vegas boasts an endless array of adventures, and we couldn't possibly cover them all. It's a city that never sleeps, and it's ever-evolving, which is part of what makes it so incredibly unique.

In Las Vegas, you'll find a world like no other, where you can explore everything from vibrant cityscapes to serene natural wonders—all in one place. The sheer diversity of activities, entertainment, and dining options is staggering, and it's a destination where you can truly have it all.

Start your Las Vegas escapades, and here is my advice to you: have a blast, create unforgettable memories, and cherish the moments that make you smile from ear to ear. Don't be afraid to venture off the beaten path, as some of the most remarkable experiences are found when you follow your curiosity.

The resorts in Las Vegas aren't just places to rest your head; they are adventures all by themselves. Dive into their unique worlds and relish every minute of your stay.

Finally, I want to extend a heartfelt thank you for joining me on this Las Vegas journey through these pages. Your enthusiasm for exploring this vibrant city is what makes it all worthwhile. So, pack your bags, get ready to roll the dice, and let Las Vegas work its magic on you. Here's to incredible adventures and unforgettable moments!

*Cheers to you and your Las Vegas adventure,*

# BONUS: LAS VEGAS TRAVEL JOURNAL

# The City Of Lights

_____
_____
_____
_____
_____
_____
_____
_____
_____
_____
_____
_____
_____

## Notes

_____
_____
_____
_____
_____

♣

# The City Of Lights

---
---
---
---
---
---
---
---
---
---
---

## Notes

---
---
---
---

♣

# The City Of Lights

_____

_____

_____

_____

_____

_____

_____

_____

_____

_____

_____

_____

_____

## Notes

_____

_____

_____

_____

♣

# The City Of Lights

_____
_____
_____
_____
_____
_____
_____
_____
_____
_____
_____
_____
_____

## Notes

_____
_____
_____
_____

♣

# The City Of Lights

---
---
---
---
---
---
---
---
---
---
---
---
---

## Notes

---
---
---
---

♣

# The City Of Lights

---
---
---
---
---
---
---
---
---
---
---
---
---
---

## Notes

---
---
---
---

♣

# The City Of Lights

_____
_____
_____
_____
_____
_____
_____
_____
_____
_____
_____
_____

## Notes

_____
_____
_____
_____

♣

# The City Of Lights

_____
_____
_____
_____
_____
_____
_____
_____
_____
_____
_____
_____

## Notes

_____
_____
_____
_____

♣

# The City Of Lights

---
---
---
---
---
---
---
---
---
---
---
---
---
---

## Notes

---
---
---
---

♣

# The City Of Lights

_____
_____
_____
_____
_____
_____
_____
_____
_____
_____
_____
_____
_____
_____

## Notes

_____
_____
_____
_____

♣

# The City Of Lights

---

---

---

---

---

---

---

---

---

---

---

---

---

---

---

## Notes

---

---

---

---

---

♣

# The City Of Lights

## Notes

♣

# The City Of Lights

_____
_____
_____
_____
_____
_____
_____
_____
_____
_____
_____
_____
_____

## Notes

_____
_____
_____
_____

♣

# The City Of Lights

_____
_____
_____
_____
_____
_____
_____
_____
_____
_____
_____
_____
_____
_____

## Notes

_____
_____
_____
_____
_____